THE ROOTS OF TERRORISM

THE ROOTS OF TERRORISM

Domestic Terrorism

Middle Eastern Terrorism

The Roots of Terrorism

What Is Terrorism?

Who Are the Terrorists?

Will Terrorism End?

THE ROOTS OF TERRORISM

Assaf Moghadam

The Fletcher School, Tufts University
and Harvard University

Series Consulting Editors

Leonard Weinberg and William L. Eubank

University of Nevada, Reno

CHELSEA HOUSE
P U B L I S H E R S
An imprint of Infobase Publishing

For my parents, for their integrity, support, and love.

The Roots of Terrorism

Copyright © 2006 by Infobase Publishing

Chelsea House
An imprint of Infobase Publishing
132 West 31st Street
New York NY 10001

Library of Congress Cataloging-in-Publication Data

Moghadam, Assaf, 1974–
   The roots of terrorism/Assaf Moghadam.
     p. cm. — (The roots of terrorism)
   Includes bibliographical references and index.
ISBN 0-7910-8307-1 (hard cover)
  1. Terrorism. I. Title. II. Series.
HV6431.M635 2005
303.6'25—dc22   2005021625

Chelsea House books are available at special discounts when purchased in bulk quantities for businesses, associations, institutions, or sales promotions. Please call our Special Sales Department in New York at (212) 967-8800 or (800) 322-8755.

You can find Chelsea House on the World Wide Web at http://www.chelseahouse.com

Series and cover design by Takeshi Takahashi

Printed in the United States of America

Bang 21C 10 9 8 7 6 5 4 3 2 1

This book is printed on acid-free paper.

All links and web addresses were checked and verified to be correct at the time of publication. Because of the dynamic nature of the web, some addresses and links may have changed since publication and may no longer be valid.

Leonard Weinberg and William L. Eubank
University of Nevada, Reno

Terrorism is hard to ignore. Almost every day television news shows, newspapers, magazines, and Websites run and re-run pictures of dramatic and usually bloody acts of violence carried out by ferocious-looking terrorists or claimed by shadowy militant groups. It is often hard not to be scared when we see people like us killed or maimed by terrorist attacks at fast food restaurants, in office buildings, on public buses and trains, or along normal-looking streets.

This kind of fear is exactly what those staging terrorist attacks hope to achieve. They want the public, especially the American public, to feel a profound sense of fear. Often the leaders of terrorist groups want the public not only to be frightened by the attack, but also angry at the government because it seems unable to protect them from these violent assaults.

This series of books for young people has two related purposes. The first is to place the events we see in context. We want young readers to know what terrorism is about: Who its perpetrators are, where they come from, and what they hope to gain by their violence. We also want to answer some basic questions about this type of violence. What is terrorism? What do we mean when we use the term? Is one man's terrorist another man's freedom fighter? Is terrorism new, a kind of asymmetrical warfare just invented at the beginning of the twenty-first century? Or, does terrorism have a long history stretching back over the centuries? Does terrorism ever end? Should we expect to face waves of terrorist violence stretching into the indefinite future?

This series' second purpose is to reduce the anxieties and fears of young readers. Getting a realistic picture of what terrorism is all about, knowing what is true and what is not true about it helps us "get a grip." Young readers will learn, we hope, what constitutes realistic concerns about the danger of terrorism versus irrational fear. By understanding the nature of the threat, we help defeat one of the terrorists' basic aims: spreading terror.

The first volume in the series, *What is Terrorism?*, by Leonard Weinberg and William L. Eubank, begins by defining the term "terrorism," then goes on to explain the immediate aims and long-term objectives of those who decide to use this unconventional form of violence. Weinberg and Eubank point out that terrorism did not begin with the 9/11 attacks on the United States. In fact, terrorist violence has a long history, one the authors trace from its religious roots in the ancient Middle East up to current times.

For those who believe that terrorist campaigns, once started, are endless, Jeffrey Ross's *Will Terrorism End?* will come as a useful antidote. Ross calls our attention to the various ways in which terrorist episodes have ended in the past. Many readers will be surprised to learn that most of the terrorist organizations that were active in Latin America, Western Europe, and the United States just a few decades ago have passed from the scene. For example, the Irish Republican Army (IRA), long active in paramilitary operations in Northern Ireland, is now in the process of turning to peaceful political participation.

Between accounts of the beginning and end of terrorism are books that approach the problem in two different ways. Dipak Gupta (*Who are the Terrorists?*) and Assaf Moghadam (*The Roots of Terrorism*) answer general questions about the origins of terrorists and terrorist organizations. Gupta provides profiles of individual terrorists and terrorist groups, in addition to exploring the issues that inspire terrorists. Moghadam, on the other hand, is concerned with the organizational and social roots of terrorism. For example: What causes people to join terrorist groups? What are the grievances that often give rise to terrorist campaigns?

If Gupta and Moghadam examine the roots of terrorism in general terms, Jack Levin and Arie Perliger's books each have a specific geographic focus. Levin's *Domestic Terrorism* brings the story close to home by describing domestic terrorist activity in the United States over the last half century. Perliger's book on *Middle Eastern Terrorism* offers an account of terrorist activity in the region of the world with which such violence is most closely identified.

Finally, we believe that young readers will come away from this series of books with a much clearer understanding of what terrorism is and what those individuals and groups who carry out terrorist attacks are like. ■

CHAPTER 1

WHAT IS TERRORISM?

The skies above the American northeast could hardly have been clearer on September 11, 2001. Weather conditions were unlikely to interfere with the safety of thousands of passengers who waited for their departures from the international airports Boston Logan, Washington Dulles, and Newark. Nineteen travelers on that bright, sunny morning, however, had no plans to land safely at their destination airports. Instead, they were determined to hijack four airliners and steer them into landmark American buildings, killing themselves along with thousands of innocent people. In the aftermath of the terrorist onslaught that came to be known as the "9/11 attacks," many Americans wondered what led the 19 suicide hijackers to sacrifice their lives in order to strike the United States

1

September 11, 2001, proved that terrorism is not confined to third-world countries in the Middle East and South America. Above, the second hijacked plane crashes into Tower 2 of the World Trade Center.

the heaviest blow since the Japanese surprise attack on Pearl Harbor 60 years earlier.

In trying to find the answer to the question "Why do they hate us?" Americans looked both abroad and inward. They sought to learn more about the Arab and Muslim societies from which the 9/11 hijackers and many other members of the al Qaeda terror network came. Some wondered whether the religion of Islam is inherently violent, given that many of the Muslim terrorists and their spiritual leaders profess to act in accordance with religious beliefs. Others wondered whether the answer to 9/11 lay in the grievances of the Muslim and Arab world. Were these terrorists motivated by their dislike for the West because of its history of colonizing the Arab Middle East? Others argued that United States policies were to blame, including U.S. possession of military bases in the heart of the Arab and Muslim world, its attempts to ensure access to cheap oil, and its strong support of Israel and authoritarian Arab regimes in the Middle East.[1] Some commentators looked for economic explanations, arguing that terrorism occurs when societies live, or are forced to live, in dire economic conditions, plagued by high unemployment and low economic growth.

This book does not provide a simple explanation of the root causes of acts of terrorism, such as the hijackings of 9/11. Instead, it contends that terrorism is a highly complex phenomenon deserving of a detailed discussion.

THE DEFINITION OF TERRORISM

For decades, experts on terrorism have attempted, much in vain, to formulate a universally accepted definition of terrorism. There are several reasons why this has been difficult. First, the meaning of terrorism has changed frequently throughout history. In some eras, *terror* has referred to an instrument used by the state; at other times, it has denoted tactics used by an organization against a state.

The word *terror*, of course, has negative connotations. Terrorists, in fact, hardly ever call themselves "terrorists." Instead, they brand themselves with more respectable terms, such as "freedom fighters," "liberators," or "armies." Terrorists view themselves as victims, driven to violent action as a result of the repressive actions of a government, a group of governments, or another community. They claim to act out of desperation and a lack of other viable alternatives to resistance against a superior enemy. Because *terrorism* is such a pejorative term, who is a "terrorist" and what constitutes "terrorism" may seem to be in the eyes of the beholder. Those who identify with the victims of a terrorist act will generally refer to the act as "terrorism" and the perpetrators as "terrorists," whereas those who sympathize with the group and its cause will find less negative labels to describe the group and the nature of its activities.

Although there is no agreed-upon definition of terrorism, there are several characteristics of terrorism that can help us to gain a better understanding of it. First, terrorism is a political concept, involving violence designed to achieve a political aim. Hence, terrorism is about "the pursuit of power, the acquisition of power, and the use of power to achieve political change."[2] The political nature of terrorism clearly distinguishes this form of violence from ordinary crime. Whereas terrorists act in the pursuit of political goals—such as the establishment of an independent state or the overthrow of a government—an ordinary criminal's motives are to seek personal and material gain.

Terrorism is designed to have far-reaching psychological effects not only on the actual targets of the terrorist attack, but on a wider audience. The Latin word *terrere*—the root of the modern word *terrorism*—means "to frighten." Indeed, terrorism is designed to instill fear beyond the immediate victim of the violence. The ancient Chinese proverb "Kill one, frighten ten thousand," perhaps best captures this fundamental aim and characteristic of terrorism.

Terrorism is perpetrated by a non-state organization rather than by a state. To be sure, states have engaged in various acts of terror, and in fact state-based terror is responsible for a significantly higher number of casualties than acts of terrorism perpetrated by organizations. However, we usually distinguish state-based violence by using the term *terror* rather than the word *terrorism*. The focus of this book will be on terrorism (i.e., political violence perpetrated by organizations, or so-called non-state actors). Where relevant and illustrative, however, we will also provide examples of terror (i.e., political violence perpetrated by the state).

Terrorists are different from other non-state actors, such as guerillas or militias. Members of terrorist organizations do not distinguish themselves in dress from other groups, or wear uniforms, and they do not carry membership cards. Terrorist organizations typically are small in size and tend to target primarily civilians and other groups not actively engaged in battle—so-called noncombatants. Guerrillas and militias, on the other hand, function as "small armies." They are composed of hundreds or thousands of fighters, and they primarily target the military forces of their enemies. Due to their size and quasi-military structure, guerrilla groups may seize and hold territory.

With these distinctions in mind, we can define terrorism as premeditated violence, or the threat of violence, in the pursuit of a political aim, perpetrated by organizations primarily against noncombatant targets, and usually aimed at influencing a wider audience through the creation of fear.[3]

WHY DOES TERRORISM MATTER?

In order to find solutions to a problem, or devise effective counter-measures, it is important to understand its causes. This is especially true for terrorism. But why should we care about terrorism to the extent that we do? The death toll from the tsunami that hit several countries in Southeast Asia and the Indian subcontinent in December 2004 is estimated at over 200,000. Should we not focus our efforts on dealing with such natural disasters that carry a much higher cost in human lives rather than on terrorism? People are more likely to die as a result of road accidents, cigarette smoke, or wars than they are from terrorism, so why does terrorism matter?

The first reason why terrorism matters is that in many countries, there are more victims of terrorism than most of us are aware of. Terrorist violence in Algeria, which broke out in 1992, killed tens of thousands of Algerians. Under Augusto Pinochet's military dictatorship in Chile, which lasted from 1973 until 1990, and in which terror was a widely used tactic, tens of thousands of innocent people were brutally tortured, and over 3,000 were killed or "disappeared." In Uganda, an estimated 300,000 people, most of them farmers, students, and shopkeepers, were killed by the death squads of dictator Idi Amin in the 1970s.[4] State-based or state-sponsored terror has occurred in many other countries, including Argentina, Cambodia, Colombia, El Salvador, Guatemala, Iran, Nigeria,

"Old" and "New" Terrorism

In recent decades, a new form of terrorist organization has appeared that is markedly different in its structure, tactics, ideologies, and aims from the traditional terrorist group. This phenomenon gave birth to the concept of "new terrorism," the most dangerous form of terrorism today.

Traditionally, terrorism has been carried out by clearly identifiable organizations usually active in a single country, either ethno-nationalist/separatist, such as the Irish Republican Army (IRA) and the Basque ETA, or left-wing/revolutionary (mainly active in Western Europe, Latin America, and Africa). While some of these traditional organizations still exist, they have been overshadowed by the more sophisticated, and dangerous, new terrorism organizations.

The traditional terrorist organizations tended to be secular, with a defined set of political objectives that were limited rather than absolute, as were their tactics. They tended to engage in selective violence against targets that symbolized the economic, political, and military power of their enemy. Trying to gain the sympathy of an outside audience, they generally attempted to minimize large-scale killings of innocent bystanders. By and large, they also claimed responsibility for their actions. Structurally, the and Peru. Often, this state-based terror is not counted in official reports about terrorism, partly because the numbers of victims are difficult to track.

We should also care about terrorism because it entails a number of "indirect costs."[5] One is the psychological impact of terrorism, which is disproportionately large in comparison to the actual damage of terrorism. Terrorism, as has been noted, instills fear in people's minds, and that discomfort is a cost in itself.

Another indirect cost of terrorism is economic losses incurred by states. The U.S. State Department, for instance, regularly urges American citizens to avoid travel to certain

traditional terrorist groups consisted of dozens to a few hundred members and the organization was hierarchical, with a clearly identifiable leadership.

New terrorism groups are less cohesive and more diffuse organizations. They are structured more as loose networks that are geographically dispersed. They tend to have more members than the traditional terrorist organizations, often ranging into the thousands.

Ideologically, the new terrorist organizations are less comprehensible but nevertheless highly motivated. Often religious in character, they tend to entertain absolute goals, and accordingly choose non-discriminatory tactics such as suicide bombings. In the aftermath of attacks, the new terrorist networks such as al Qaeda often refrain from claiming responsibility. The new terrorism—because of its often religious nature—is far more lethal than traditional terrorism. Today, the most dangerous manifestation of the new terrorism is its radical Islamist variant, which targets all countries that do not conform to its fanatical worldview. Their absolute devotion to their cause, and their absolute demands (which are difficult to fulfill), make the new terrorists difficult to deter or appease.

high-risk regions, warnings that create high economic losses for those countries. Similarly, businesses may need to reevaluate financial investments in countries that are considered possible targets of terrorism. These companies may be forced to spend more money on security measures, which raises the cost of investments, and may deter businesses from investing in those countries.

Another indirect cost is counter-terrorism measures. In its annual budget, the Clinton administration spent $10 billion on counter-terrorism—money that otherwise could have been used to improve education, build roads, or provide a better health care system. Increasing the physical defenses of a country around critical infrastructure such as airports, embassies, ports, and nuclear power plants—a measure known as *hardening*—is another obvious economic cost of terrorism.

Terrorism also sets back major peace processes, thus creating instability in the international system. Terrorist attacks have contributed to the derailment of the Israeli–Palestinian and Northern Ireland peace processes, to name only two examples, and are thus a threat to world peace in a way that other forms of violence, including crime, are not.[6]

AN INCREASING THREAT

Now, at the beginning of the twenty-first century, it has become increasingly clear that terrorism is a major threat to the security and interests not only of Americans, but of citizens of other countries. Developments of the early 1990s increased the potential damage that terrorism can inflict. Nuclear weapons, materials, and information have become more accessible, and could fall into the hands of countries or organizations that harbor aggressive intentions toward others, a problem generally referred to as "loose nukes." A region of particular concern is the former Soviet Union, where there is evidence of a black market in uranium and plutonium, materials that can be used to produce nuclear bombs. Russian authorities, for instance, have apparently foiled hundreds of nuclear-material smuggling deals. Furthermore, there is concern that former Soviet nuclear scientists will sell their valuable skills to terrorist organizations.[7]

Another troubling scenario is that highly lethal chemical or biological weapons could fall into the hands of terrorist organizations. In 1995, the Japanese sect Aum Shinrikyo became the first terrorist group to use nerve gas on a large scale, when they released sarin into the Tokyo subway, killing 12 people and injuring 5,000 others. Future acquisition of chemical or biological weapons by terrorists is now a major concern of policymakers.

While terrorists who possess chemical, biological, and nuclear weapons can create an immense amount of damage, terrorists do face significant obstacles in the production and dissemination of such weapons of mass destruction (WMD). In addition, terrorists often favor other, more proven methods of destruction. So, while the specter of WMD in the hands of terrorists is very troublesome, it is by no means certain that terrorists will be successful in staging a WMD attack in the near future.

The spread of modern means of communication, especially the Internet, has also increased the threat of terrorism. The Internet has allowed groups with a propensity toward violence to freely and widely distribute guidance on how to manufacture bombs, how to produce chemical or biological weapons, and how to act surreptitiously when preparing for an attack. The increasing reliance of modern societies on information technology has also given rise to another terrorist threat referred to as "cyberterrorism"—that is, an attack on computer networks by terrorist organizations.

The global resurgence of religion since the 1990s has increased the threat level and lethality of terrorism.[8] The rise of religiousness has been accompanied by a rise in religiously-motivated terrorism, and has been used to justify particularly costly and brutal forms of violence (see Chapter 7).

EXAMINING THE CAUSES OF TERRORISM

Terrorism is a phenomenon that cannot be examined in isolation. Indeed, it is a complex concept that is best understood in a larger context. A clear understanding of terrorism requires insights from a variety of disciplines, including political science, international relations, psychology, sociology, religious studies, cultural studies, and economics.

In this book, the roots of terrorism will be examined from three different but equally essential perspectives.[9] The first is the individual perspective, which will focus on the psychology of the person who joins or leads the terrorist group. We will examine whether or not terrorists are mentally ill and how individual terrorists justify the use of violence against civilians who are not engaged in battle against them. The focus will then shift to some of the psychological mechanisms that occur once the individual joins the terrorist group, and how group dynamics affect his or her behavior.

The second perspective from which the causes of terrorism will be examined is the organizational perspective. Understanding terrorist organizations is fundamental to our grasp of why terrorism occurs, because the overwhelming majority of terrorist acts are perpetrated by organizations, not by individuals acting alone. Organizations provide the infrastructure, the means, the ideology, the justification, and the social support required to carry out terrorist activities. In addition, terrorist organizations have to engage in acts of violence for reasons that are particular to the group, including the need to survive as an organization.

We will also examine terrorism from a third perspective, that of the larger environment. Many environmental factors and conditions provide the context for the organization and the individual engaged in terrorism. Political, social, economic, and other conditions affect organizations and individuals, and have an impact on their decisions to commit acts of violence to achieve their goals, rather than seeking nonviolent

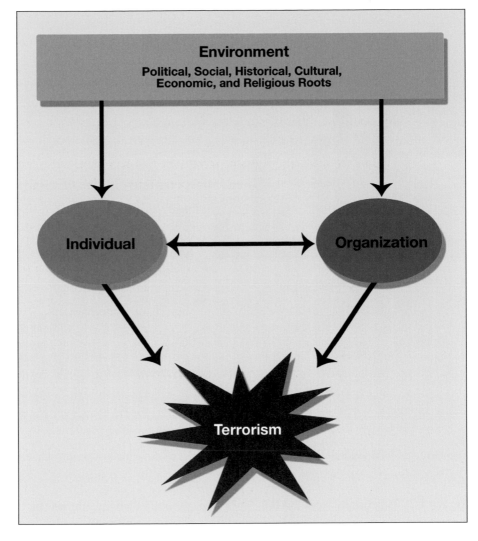

Figure 1.1 The Causes of Terrorism: Three Perspectives. This chart demonstrates the factors that contribute to terrorism.

means. Environmental factors include political motivations, such as the aspiration for national independence; economic motivations, such as poverty; and societal aspects, such as class differences within a given group or community. We will also look at whether or not a particular community's culture and history affect its decisions to employ terrorism. Finally, this

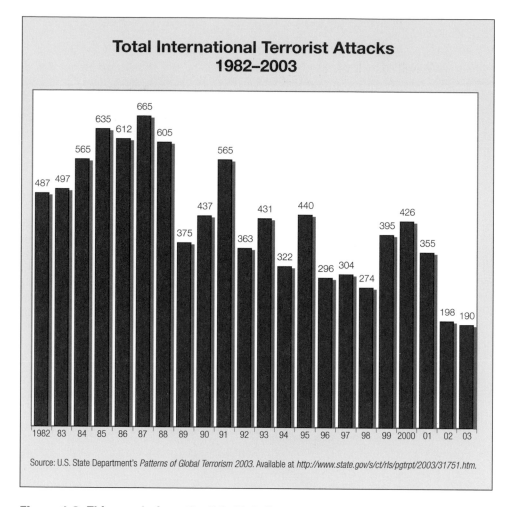

**Total International Terrorist Attacks
1982–2003**

Source: U.S. State Department's *Patterns of Global Terrorism 2003*. Available at *http://www.state.gov/s/ct/rls/pgtrpt/2003/31751.htm*.

**Figure 1.2 This graph, from the U.S. State Department's Website, shows the
total number of international terrorist attacks per year over two decades.**

book will examine religious causes of terrorism throughout
history. It will establish that nearly all religious groups have
engaged in acts of terrorism at some point in their histories.

The main argument of this book is that a multitude of
factors exist that can give rise to terrorism and that simple
explanations are unsatisfactory. This broad overview of the
roots of terrorism is designed to stimulate appreciation of
the complexities of this social phenomenon while disabusing

the reader from commonly held yet erroneous beliefs that there are easy explanations for terrorism.

We will also look at the causes of terrorism throughout history. For that reason, some examples used to illustrate various theories about the causes of terrorism are drawn from terrorist groups that are no longer active. However, the lessons we may learn from these examples remain urgent and relevant.

CHAPTER 2

PSYCHOLOGICAL EXPLANATIONS OF TERRORISM

On May 9, 1976, two guards opened Cell No. 719 at Germany's high-security prison, Stuttgart-Stammheim, to discover the dead body of Europe's most notorious female terrorist, Ulrike Meinhof. Meinhof's suicide by strangulation put an end to the turbulent life of a young and prominent German journalist who, in her mid 30s, chose to replace her pen with a bomb. Meinhof was a member of Germany's notorious Baader-Meinhof Gang and was one of the founders of Germany's radical anarchist Red Army Faction (RAF), which spread fear and terror in West Germany during the 1970s.

When Meinhof was buried a week after her death, few among the funeral attendees knew that one organ of her body—her brain— was absent. In 1962, well before her descent into the terrorist

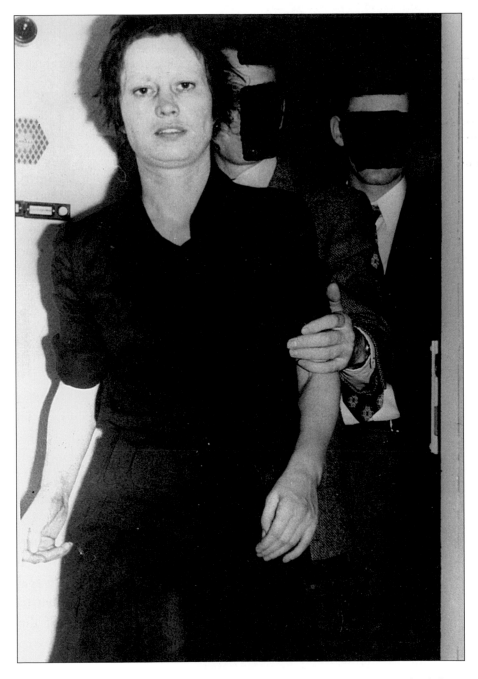

Ulrike Meinhof is taken into custody, as shown here. Meinhof was the joint head of the West German left-wing Baader-Meinhof terrorist gang, and became one of the founders of the radical anarchist Red Army Faction.

underground, Meinhof had undergone brain surgery to remove a benign tumor. After her suicide 14 years later, a neuropathologist was asked to remove Meinhof's brain for study. German authorities were interested not only in whether Meinhof's earlier brain surgery had played a role in pushing her into terrorism, but also in learning more about the mind of the terrorist.

The question of whether or not there is a "terrorist mindset" has occupied terrorism researchers, psychologists, and psychiatrists for decades. This chapter looks at the current research into the psychological aspects of terrorism. Among the questions that will be discussed are the following: Are terrorists mentally ill? What psychological explanations have researchers produced to explain terrorism and the "mind of the terrorist"? What are the psychological processes through which terrorists justify the use of violence? What are the psychological dynamics between the individual and the terrorist group?

It may come as a surprise to some readers that our current understanding about the psychology of terrorists is relatively limited, mainly because research has proven extremely difficult to conduct. Terrorism analysts and psychologists have very little access to terrorists since, due to the nature of their illegal activities, terrorists tend to live clandestinely or are held under arrest. In addition, governments often restrict access to incarcerated terrorists because of security concerns. When researchers do manage to interview terrorists, the latter may provide a highly distorted description of their activities or even deliberately mislead the interviewer in an attempt to present their actions in a positive light or avoid revealing the terrorist organization's secrets.

ARE TERRORISTS MENTALLY ILL?

Terrorism analysts, government officials, and neuroscientists have long wondered whether the dark and dangerous lifestyle of terrorists—a lifestyle prone to aggression and violence—

is the result of a mental illness afflicting the individual. Do terrorists suffer from mental disorders and, if so, can such an illness be diagnosed and cured? The advantage in identifying a psychological abnormality in terrorists, if one exists, is obvious: It would help governments to spot terrorists in advance and thus help prevent attacks and save countless innocent lives.

Modern psychiatry distinguishes between two major classes of behavioral disorders. Axis I includes major clinical illnesses such as schizophrenia, psychosis, and major depression. Individuals suffering from Axis I psychiatric disorders are considered unable to distinguish right from wrong. Axis II disorders consist of so-called personality disorders such as sociopathy or antisocial personality disorders. Individuals suffering from Axis II disorders are considered to be able to distinguish between right and wrong, yet they choose wrong for selfish reasons and without qualms of conscience.[10]

There is a relatively broad consensus among psychologists and psychiatrists that most terrorists are not insane or mentally ill, and not even sociopathic. In other words, save for some rare exceptions, most terrorists suffer from neither Axis I nor Axis II disorders and are therefore not considered mentally ill.[11] "This failure of mental illness as an explanation for terrorism," psychiatrist Marc Sageman states, "is consistent with three decades of research that has been unable to detect any significant pattern of mental illness in terrorists."[12]

Most researchers agree that terrorists, while highly alienated from society, are sane and relatively normal in the sense that they do not exhibit a striking psychopathology.[13] Indeed, schizophrenics and other individuals with mental illnesses would have difficulties functioning in group settings. On the premise that it requires a group effort to be able to stage highly sophisticated terrorist attacks, rational terrorist leaders would thus avoid recruiting mentally ill individuals who could jeopardize attacks and endanger the survival of the group.[14]

Rather than viewing terrorists as mentally ill, a more useful and accurate description would be that of terrorists as fanatics, an approach that "views the terrorist as a cool, logical planning individual whose rewards are ideological and political. . . ."[15] Fanaticism entails an unwillingness to compromise and an inclination to see things in terms of "black and white." Fanatics are close-minded and disdain views with which they disagree. Trying to understand terrorists as fanatics is advantageous because it does not contradict the fact that many terrorists are indeed highly sophisticated and educated.

CONTENDING PSYCHOLOGICAL THEORIES OF TERRORISM

Some psychiatrists and psychologists who believe that a tendency toward terrorism is innate rather than acquired have advanced a number of theories claiming that terrorists may be influenced by psychological traits and motives in making their decisions to join terrorist organizations. According to neurologist and psychiatrist Jeff Victoroff, these psychological theories on terrorism can be divided into three categories: psychoanalytic, nonpsychoanalytic, and group theories of terrorism.[16]

Psychoanalytic Theories

Psychoanalytic theories on terrorism have their origin in the studies of the Austrian neurologist Sigmund Freud (1856–1939). Contemporary psychologists that fall into this school—so-called neo-Freudians—assume that much of mental life is unconscious; that psychological development proceeds in stages based on childhood sexual fantasies; and that psychological distress derives from unresolved internal conflict related to these fantasies. Three prominent sub-theories of psychoanalytic approaches to terrorism are identity theory, narcissism theory, and paranoia theory.

According to identity theory, individuals who are prone to terrorism are young, lack self-esteem, and have a strong need to consolidate their identities.[17] Narcissism theory emphasizes the need of infants to be loved in order to develop normally.

Failure of the mother to provide the infant with empathy damages the self-image, resulting in what is known as narcissistic injuries. Such injuries, in turn, produce narcissistic rage, which lead the wounded individual to seek to destroy the source of the narcissistic injury.[18]

According to paranoia theory, extensively advanced by Dr. Jerrold Post of Georgetown University, people suffering from paranoid personality disorders exhibit a pervasive distrust and suspicion of others, to whom they ascribe malicious motives. Dr. Post believes that individuals with certain personality traits are disproportionately attracted to terrorist careers. These individuals tend to be action-oriented excitement-seekers, aggressive personalities, or people who have had little success in their lives.

Terrorists, according to Dr. Post, have often shown signs of what psychologists call "externalization" and "splitting," commonly found in narcissistic personality disturbances. Splitting involves individuals who have been subjected to some form of psychological damage (narcissistic wounds) during childhood. The result is that these individuals develop a "damaged self-concept," in which the "good" and the "bad" parts of the self are in conflict. Dr. Post explains that a person with such wounds "idealizes his grandiose self" and externalizes or "projects onto others all the hated and devalued weakness within."[19] Such individuals often need an outside enemy to blame. This is one reason why terrorists tend to divide the world into "black and white" or "us versus them," which helps them identify their enemies as the source of all problems. Dr. Post calls this terrorist logic the "psycho-logic," which dictates to the mentally disturbed terrorist that if "they" (the Other) "are the source of our problems," then "they" must be destroyed.[20] Hence, the terrorist's zeal represents his eagerness to destroy the devalued and disowned part of the self.[21]

Nonpsychoanalytic Theories

The second major category of psychological explanations of terrorism consists of nonpsychoanalytic theories. Three prominent nonpsychoanalytic theories are novelty-seeking, cognitive, and humiliation-revenge theories. According to novelty-seeking theory, political violence may satisfy innate and possibly genetically-determined needs for stimulation and risk at high levels.[22]

Cognitive theories of terrorism are connected to an individual's cognitive capacity, which "refers to mental functions such as memory, attention, concentration, language, and the so-called 'executive' functions, including the capacity to learn and follow rules, to anticipate outcomes, to make sensible inferences, and to perform accurate risk-benefit calculations."[23] A large number of these mental operations are carried out within a part of the brain known as the dorsolateral prefrontal cortex, which attends to how individuals perceive specific circumstances. While more research needs to be done in this field, there is substantial evidence that violent behavior, including that of leaders, is influenced by an individual's cognitive capacity.

A third nonpsychoanalytic theory of terrorism is humiliation-revenge theory, which argues that humiliation may serve as a source of intense anger, leading the humiliated individual to desire a retaliation against individuals or other targets associated with the entity believed responsible for the humiliation.[24] In forensic psychiatry and criminology, the association between humiliation and a passion for revenge is well known and likely to contribute to many ordinary criminal murders.[25]

THE TERRORIST'S JUSTIFICATION OF VIOLENCE

Psychology can also be used as a tool to better understand how terrorists justify and rationalize the use of violence. What are the psychological processes that enable terrorists to use violence? Why do some individuals engage in violence while others don't?

Psychologist Albert Bandura has provided a convincing answer to these questions. He explains that when ordinary individuals interact in their daily lives, they abide by certain codes of behaviors or moral standards. These moral standards

PSYCHOLOGICAL THEORIES OF TERRORISM

Theory	Main Motives for Terrorist's Use of Violence
Identity Theory	Young and lacking in self-esteem, the terrorist harbors a need to strengthen his or her identity.
Narcissism Theory	Lack of empathy (e.g., from parents) creates narcissistic injury and a desire to harm the source of that injury.
Paranoia Theory	Acute distrust and suspicion of others, who are perceived as evil and harmful. The terrorist's struggle is in reality one against his own "bad self."
Cognitive Theory	Diminished mental functions such as memory, attention, concentration, language, ability to learn and follow rules and/or make sensible decisions increase the likelihood that an individual will engage in violence.
Novelty-Seeking Theory	Innate aspects of temperament, such as aggression, the need for thrill and excitement, and risk-taking.
Humiliation-Revenge Theory	Humiliation by an oppressive state or community creates internal pressure to take revenge against the source of the humiliation.
Theories of Group Process	Group forces, such as ideological indoctrination, repetitive training, peer pressure, and the lifting of constraints influence the decision to perpetrate acts of terrorism.

Table 2.1 Are terrorists mentally ill? While the general consensus is that they are not, there are a variety of psychological theories that might be used to analyze individual terrorists.

are what he calls "self-sanctions," because they help prevent the individual from behaving in a way that may offend other people.

There are, however, several ways in which individuals can gradually remove these self-sanctions, a process Dr. Bandura calls "mechanisms of moral disengagement." One such mechanism is moral justification, when aggressive behavior is portrayed as serving a moral purpose. Moral justifications for wars have been extremely common in the history of Judaism, Christianity, and Islam, as we shall see in Chapter 7.

A second mechanism is labeling reprehensible activities in respectable and positive terms. There are many contemporary examples of such positive labeling, including the term *collateral damage*, which is used to describe accidental damage to civilians, property, or territory during violent conflict. The term *collateral damage* may mask the very real suffering that terrorist groups or national armies inflict on innocent men, women, and children who happened to be in the wrong place at the wrong time. Another example of euphemistic labeling is the term *ethnic cleansing*, which became popular in the 1990s during the breakup of the former Yugoslavia. The term refers to the expulsion of an undesirable population from a particular territory due to religious or ethnic discrimination, political, strategic or ideological considerations, or a combination of these factors. The removal may take the form of population transfer, deportation, systematic rape, and, at times, genocide (the deliberate killing of members of a certain national, ethnic, racial, or religious community).

A third mechanism used to justify violence is when the terrorist group places its own violent acts in a relatively positive light by contrasting them with the inhumanities of another, often opposing, group. Terrorists will often attempt to marginalize their gruesome deeds by pointing out that they have no other means left to defend themselves against cruelties inflicted on their people. A comment by Ramadan Shalah, a leader of the Palestinian Islamic Jihad (PIJ), a group that has staged dozens of suicide terrorist attacks in Israel, illustrates this point: "We have nothing with which to repel killing and thuggery against us except the weapon of martyrdom. . . . It is easy and costs us only our lives . . . human bombs cannot be defeated, not even by nuclear bombs."[26]

A particularly widespread and effective way in which moral inhibitions are reduced is the use of so-called dehumanization, when people or groups divest their enemies of human qualities, such as by referring to them as monkeys, pigs, and worms. During Germany's Third Reich period, Jews were dehumanized in various ways. Nazi Germans, for instance, referred to Jews almost exclusively in singular form as "The Jew" to deprive Jews of their individualism and, by extension, their humanity. Shaving the heads of Jewish inmates upon their arrival at labor and death camps served a similar purpose. As Dr. Bandura states, "once dehumanized, the potential victims are no longer viewed as persons with feelings, hopes, and concerns but as subhuman objects."[27] Studies of aggression have confirmed that it is easier to mistreat people once they are dehumanized.

THE TERRORIST AND THE GROUP

The terrorist group influences the psychology of its individual members in several ways. Membership in the group itself provides the terrorist with a sense of belonging, purpose, perceived social status, and empowerment that he would otherwise not enjoy. The individual may join the terrorist group because he views the rewards of joining as highly satisfying. Terrorist organizations can provide the individual an opportunity for excitement, glamour, and fame, as well as a chance of demonstrating his or her courage. Groups also provide the individual with an opportunity to avenge personal humiliations.

Once the individual has joined the organization, he becomes a member of a larger cause, and his freedom of action is increasingly restricted. The group provides the terrorist with a belief system that elevates the organization's goals above the

(continued on page 26)

Patty Hearst is photographed here in front of the flag used by her kidnappers, members of the Symbionese Liberation Army. Hearst is infamous for her conversion from victim to seemingly willing accomplice.

Patty Hearst and the Symbionese Liberation Army

On April 15, 1974, four armed women and a man entered the Hibernia Bank in the Sunset district of San Francisco, robbing the bank of $10,000 in less than four minutes. It was no ordinary bank robbery. One of the women was soon identified on videotape as Patricia ("Patty") Campbell Hearst, the granddaughter of William Randolph Hearst, a legendary media mogul.

Two months prior to the bank robbery, Hearst, a 19-year-old college student, had been kidnapped from her Berkeley apartment by members of the self-described Symbionese Liberation Army (SLA). The group said it wanted to start a revolution of the disadvantaged classes, and their main targets were wealthy and privileged individuals such as the Hearst family.

To the amazement of the police and the public at large, Hearst appeared to be a willing participant in the bank robbery. In addition, the SLA released several tapes in which she appeared increasingly sympathetic to the group's agenda. The transformation seemed complete when the Hearst family received a photo of Patty—who now called herself "Tania"—holding a rifle while standing in front of the SLA's logo, a seven-headed cobra. In one of the tapes released shortly after the bank robbery, she called her parents "pigs" and stated "I am a soldier of the people's army." Hearst seemed to show signs of "Stockholm Syndrome"—a psychological state whereby a person detained against his or her free will, including the victim of a kidnapping, may develop a sympathetic relationship with the captor(s).

Hearst was eventually arrested in September 1975. During the trial, her defense team argued that she had been brainwashed and Hearst reported that she had been held in isolation, told that she might die, and that nobody was going to rescue her. Added to her trauma were apparent physical and sexual abuses by several members of the gang. The prosecution argued instead that Hearst was a willing participant, a "rebel with a cause."

Hearst was sentenced to a multiyear prison term. After serving 21 months, President Jimmy Carter commuted her sentence under strict terms. In January 2001, President Clinton pardoned Hearst for her role in the bank robbery. The mystery of her transformation under the SLA, meanwhile, has never been fully solved.

(continued from page 23)
personal goals of each member. Other processes within the group, such as repetitive training and peer pressure, further reduce some of the terrorist's moral self-sanctions that might ordinarily prevent him from using violence. The group also frees the individual member of his personal responsibility if and when the individual engages in an act of terrorism.

Smaller and more cohesive terrorist groups, like the radical left-wing groups that were dominant in Western Europe in the late 1960s and 1970s, often impose conformity and demand complete subservience of the group member to the organization's goal. Members are often prohibited from forming relations with people outside of the group. Small terrorist groups, which often resemble cults, at times subject their members to thought control or "brainwashing."[28]

In terrorist groups, the decision-making process of the individual is strongly subordinate to the group. When highly cohesive groups make decisions, often under stress, they tend to display the characteristics of what Irving Janis called "groupthink," a concept related to the dynamics of peer pressure and group solidarity.[29] Groups that show symptoms of groupthink often have illusions of invulnerability, believe that their decisions are moral, and exercise pressure on other members of the group to think with one mind. The result of groupthink is poor decision-making that results from excessive optimism and risk-taking, an unwillingness to accept dissenting voices, and negative perceptions about their enemies.

Many of these group dynamics were apparent in Aum Shinrikyo, the Japanese cult best known for its release of sarin nerve gas in the Tokyo subway system on March 20, 1995. A doomsday cult, Aum Shinrikyo, which in 2000 changed its name to Aleph, was obsessed with the apocalypse. The group was centered around its founder and leader, Shoko Asahara, who preached to his disciples that the end of the world was near.

Asahara was born in 1955, blind in one eye and with diminished vision in his other eye. He was sent to a boarding school for the blind where, thanks to his limited ability to see, he was able to assume a leadership role. Asahara became a dominant and aggressive bully, extorting money from and spreading fear among his blind classmates. In 1984, Asahara created a Yoga center called Aum, Inc., and a year later began to present himself as a holy figure with mystical powers. By 1987, Asahara was clearly megalomaniacal (suffering from a mental disorder involving delusions of personal grandeur) and began to develop a personality cult around himself.

By the mid 1980s, Asahara had about 3,000 followers. In order to assume control over the lives of his disciples he instituted strict behavior policies. Many of the new recruits were required to donate their entire belongings to what was then Aum Shinrikyo. The cult used various methods of thought control to assume complete power over its members, including extremely brutal forms of physical and psychological abuse and extensive use of LSD and other hallucinogenic drugs. The slightest transgressions of Shoko Asahara's disciples were met with severe punishment, including drugging, sleep and food deprivation, and forced baths in ice cold and/or boiling hot water. The most extreme transgression—the desire to abandon the group—was punishable by death.[30]

People often join terrorist groups because of their desire to belong, and Aum Shinrikyo was particularly successful in attracting Japanese men and women who felt lost and alienated in Japan's rigid, hard-working, and increasingly materialistic society. Young, alienated students of the so-called hard sciences such as biology, chemistry, and physics, as well as medical students and computer geeks, found a great appeal in the teachings of a cult that promised them an escape from the pressures and hardships of everyday life.

SUMMARY

Psychological research is important to the study of terrorism and can provide insights into motivations of the individual terrorist, the way that terrorists justify the use of violence, and the dynamics of the terrorist group.

The belief that terrorists are insane can be an emotionally satisfying explanation for those wondering how individuals are capable of perpetrating acts of violence for political goals. Nonetheless, decades of psychological and psychiatric research on terrorism has shown that, except for isolated cases, terrorists are not mentally ill. Instead, as Professor Martha Crenshaw, a leading terrorism expert, has concluded, the "outstanding common characteristic of terrorists is their normality."[31] This makes sense because terrorist groups are dependent upon "sane" members who are able to carefully plan and execute attacks while maintaining a calm demeanor. Terrorists must be able to perpetrate their horrendous activities in a way that will not arouse suspicion, and it is difficult to imagine how a mentally ill terrorist would succeed in doing this.

A more plausible approach is to think of terrorists as fanatics and extremists. Terrorists are prone to violent action because of a relentless and single-minded belief in certain ideologies and values. Terrorists also seem to be heavily influenced by intense feelings of hatred, revulsion, revenge, and envy.[32]

Psychology has been invaluable in helping us understand how terrorists and terrorist groups make decisions. Psychological explanations have also been particularly important in shedding light on some of the internal group dynamics in a high-stress environment, such as that of a terrorist group, and how these dynamics affect the individual member.

Terrorist organizations are predominantly structured as hierarchies, with clear distinctions between the leadership, followers, and a range of intermediate roles. These different roles that individuals fill within the terrorist organization may attract people with different psychological backgrounds. So, it is unlikely that a single psychological profile of a terrorist will ever be identified.

Psychological factors alone do not explain the genesis of terrorism; various other factors need to be taken into account. Organizational and group dynamics seem especially important in understanding the causes of terrorism, and we will take a closer look at terrorist organizations, their structures, and their goals, in the next chapter. A purely psychological perspective also disregards the larger societal aspects of terrorism. Environmental and social factors such as economics, modernization, culture, religion, and nationalism play a large role in understanding the roots of terrorism, and these aspects will be discussed in later chapters.

CHAPTER 3

ORGANIZATIONAL EXPLANATIONS OF TERRORISM

While the psychology of an individual may play an important role, terrorism is not usually the outcome of certain personality types or mental illnesses. Instead, as a leading terrorism expert has concluded, "terrorism is primarily a group activity."[33] In this chapter, we will take a closer look at the roots of terrorism from an organizational perspective.[34]

Terrorism is rarely carried out by individuals acting on their own. It is instead conducted by members of more or less identifiable organizations, groups, or smaller cells that form part of a larger network of groups. Suicide bombings in Israel, for instance, have been carried out by members of Hamas, Palestinian Islamic Jihad (PIJ), Al Aqsa Martyrs Brigade, and the Popular Front for the Liberation of Palestine (PFLP).

This Palestinian girl wears a suicide bomber belt during a rally held by Hamas in September 2002. Many suicide bombings in Israel have been carried out by members of Hamas and other Islamist/nationalist groups.

Only in sporadic cases have individuals acted on their own. Even the most highly motivated suicide bomber will ordinarily lack the financial resources, technical know-how, and precise information that is needed to stage a successful attack. It is the organization that has the wherewithal to provide the required expertise, resources, and intelligence.[35]

Terrorist organizations are a particular type of political organization. Their distinguishing feature, as compared with common political organizations such as political parties or nonprofit interest groups, is that they rely on violence to achieve their political aims. Due to their conspiratorial nature, members of terrorist organizations must be able to maintain secrecy if they want to resist the government's effort to defeat them. Survival is the fundamental goal of any political organization and, like other political groups, terrorist organizations hence strive to maintain themselves.[36]

Al Qaeda

It was not long after the horrific attacks of 9/11 that the U.S. government credited al Qaeda (Arabic for "the Base") with the most devastating acts of terrorism ever carried out on U.S. soil. What is al Qaeda and what kind of organization, if any, does it represent?

Al Qaeda grew out of an organization called the Services Bureau (Mektab al-Khidmat, or MAK). The MAK was established in Afghanistan in 1984 by Osama bin Laden and his former teacher, Abdullah Azzam. The idea behind the MAK was to recruit and train Arab Muslims who wanted to fight the Soviet Army, which had invaded Afghanistan in 1979. In 1988, Osama bin Laden conceived of the idea that became al Qaeda, a vision of a multinational army of Muslim soldiers that could be drawn upon whenever Muslims were believed to be under attack. The MAK and the early al Qaeda had a clear hierarchical structure typical of traditional organizations, including a top leadership and committees responsible for training, logistics, military, intelligence, and media and propaganda.

Bin Laden never intended for al Qaeda to remain an ordinary organization, however; he wanted to expand it into a multinational network of organizations. By the mid 1990s—aided by modern information technology—al Qaeda was able to expand its presence to Africa, Asia, Europe, the Persian Gulf, and East Asia. It had also created more or less formal relationships with a number of terrorist organizations, thus laying the groundwork for a true global terrorist network. While al Qaeda's core continued to be hierarchically structured until shortly after 9/11, it placed considerable emphasis on creating a transnational structure. It would be wrong to assume that al Qaeda controlled the network it helped create. Rather than steering the other groups in the network, it exerted influence on them by providing funding, advice, and contacts.

ORGANIZATIONAL MOTIVES FOR TERRORISM

The very goal of survival that the terrorist organization strives for can motivate the group to commit acts of terrorism. Survival of the organization is important not only for those members

Al Qaeda's core was destroyed in the aftermath of September 11, 2001, and it effectively ceased to be a functioning organization. Although al Qaeda has retained highly skilled operatives, it is best understood as a transnational terrorist movement with no headquarters, but many local representatives loosely linked to a radical Islamist (or jihadist) ideology. These local representatives do not necessarily coordinate their activities. Nevertheless, they are bound by a common worldview that preaches the need to wage a global jihad against all "non-believers," including not only Christians and Jews, but also Muslims that do not agree with this movement's core principles.

The Iraq war that began in March 2003 and the insurgency that followed demonstrated al Qaeda's ability to adapt and expand by absorbing new organizations into the larger movement. One radical Islamist organization that merged with al Qaeda in the midst of the war was Abu Musab al-Zarqawi's group *Al Tawhid w'al Jihad* (Unity and Jihad) which, after joining al Qaeda, subsequently changed its name to "Al Qaeda in the Land of the Two Rivers," in reference to the Iraqi rivers Euphrates and Tigris.

In the years after the 9/11 attacks, the traditional al Qaeda organization has become a worldview that attracts a growing number of Muslims around the world. It is a radical international ideology with a large number of followers, few of whom are directly linked to Osama bin Laden or his associates. They are, however, followers of bin Laden in that they adhere to his methods and ideology, and they copy his style. This international movement of radical Islamists is more aptly labeled "global jihad" than "al Qaeda," and it is a phenomenon that is likely to continue to pose a threat to the United States and other countries in the foreseeable future.

who have joined the group for purely ideological reasons, but perhaps even more so for those members who have joined the organization for personal reasons. Terrorists who join due to a sense of belonging or to seek comradeship, social status, empowerment, or financial rewards have much to lose if the terrorist organization ceases to exist, because it will put an end to the benefits for which they joined the group.

The organizational tendency to maintain itself usually comes to the fore when the group's leaders decide to make drastic changes in tactics. In terrorist groups, drastic changes in the organization's strategy may include the renunciation of violence, the organization's participation in peace negotiations, or an announcement that the formerly outlawed group seeks legitimacy by turning itself into a law-abiding political party. The result of such an organizational sea change may be the formation of so-called "offshoots"—smaller and usually more radical factions that split from the main group to form a self-standing organization.

The case of the Irish Republican Army (IRA) illustrates this point. The highly complex conflict in Northern Ireland, which is partly about national identity, partly about political determination, and partly religious, has pitted two groups against each other. On one side are the overwhelmingly Catholic "Nationalists," who generally want the British province of Northern Ireland to become part of Ireland. The Nationalists form a minority of about 40 percent of the population of Northern Ireland. On the other side are the overwhelmingly Protestant "Unionists," who form the majority of about 60 percent of the Northern Irish population. The Unionists believe that the province of Northern Ireland, which has been a part of the United Kingdom since 1921, should remain loyal to the British crown.

The most prominent Catholic Nationalist group is the IRA, which has used violence to achieve several goals: the withdrawal of British troops from Northern Ireland; the political unification of Ireland through the merger of Ulster province with the Republic of Ireland; and the creation of a socialist republic in a united Ireland. While there have been various generations of the IRA, it has been officially known as the "Provisional IRA" (PIRA) since 1969.

In 1997, the PIRA announced a cease-fire as part of peace talks that eventually led to the Good Friday (Belfast) Agreement of 1998. The PIRA's decision to join peace talks, and to begin a process of disarming, led to the formation of a splinter group that called itself the Real IRA (RIRA). The RIRA denounced the PIRA leadership, accusing them of betraying the cause of forming a unified Irish state separate from the United Kingdom. The RIRA issued a statement that it would continue the armed struggle that the PIRA had denounced in the Belfast peace talks, and it soon made good on its promise by staging some of the most brutal terrorist attacks in the history of the Northern Ireland conflict, such as the Omagh Bombing.

Organizational survival may have been one of the reasons that members of PIRA decided to break off and form RIRA, the more radical offshoot that would continue the violent struggle. Splits occur in most terrorist organizations at some point. It is often the result of a struggle between "hard-liners" and "moderates" within a group, or the outcome of personal ambitions of individual members. Splits may also occur when younger generations of militants feel that they are not well represented in the group's leadership. Finally, splits may occur because, as Walter Laqueur has pointed out, "for at least some terrorists the struggle is more important than the attainment of the aim. For this reason . . . the struggle must never end."[37]

Beyond organizational survival, a terrorist organization is motivated to act because of its ideological purpose. Left-wing terrorist groups that subscribe to Marxist and Communist ideology, such as the German Red Army Faction, the Italian Red Brigades, or the French organization Action Directe, perceive their attacks as part of a class struggle in which the exploited masses that they ostensibly represent will eventually gain the upper hand. Religious terrorist movements are driven by a religious ideology. In 1984, for example, the Makhteret, or Jewish Underground, attempted to blow up the Dome of the Rock, a Muslim holy shrine located on Jerusalem's Temple Mount. Among their goals was to set off a world war that would eventually lead to the redemption of the Jewish people.

A third motivation for an organization to commit acts of terrorism can be its rivalry with other terrorist organizations. An organization may stage a terrorist attack or adopt a particular terrorist tactic, such as hijacking or suicide bombing, mainly in order to increase its popularity vis-à-vis another terrorist group or groups. For example, Palestinian terrorist organizations that have employed tactics of suicide bombings have been able to increase public support and hence their ability to recruit new members to their organizations. Adopting this particularly gruesome tactic has helped these groups attain legitimacy, which in turn has assisted them in their struggle for leadership in the territories under Palestinian control.[38]

STRATEGIC CALCULATIONS

Terrorism can be understood as a deliberate choice made by an organization that believes that violence is the best means to advance its political goals. For the terrorist group, therefore, its actions will appear to be "rational."[39]

Ordinary political organizations have a variety of options at their disposal to pursue their aims. Political parties, for example, offer themselves for elections in representative bodies such as parliaments and assemblies. Interest groups such as People for the Ethical Treatment of Animals (PETA) stage rallies, demonstrations, and other public campaigns to express their views. Terrorist organizations may use some of the means that parties or interest groups use, such as issuing leaflets or posting propaganda on the Internet. A growing number of terrorist groups have their own Websites. Terrorist groups differ from ordinary political organizations, however, in their belief that violence is the main method or strategy to see that their political goals are met.

In determining when to stage attacks, terrorist organizations may be guided by a variety of calculations. Groups may decide to adopt terrorist methods after they have tried a number of different means. One political group that initially refrained from the use of violence, but then gradually adopted terrorist tactics, was the American organization the Weathermen (also known as the Weather Underground), which derived its name from the lyrics of a Bob Dylan song: "You don't need a weatherman to know which way the wind blows." The Weathermen emerged out of an initially peaceful and nonviolent "New Left" movement. By 1969, however, following a number of violent confrontations with the police, the group decided to adopt terrorist tactics. In 1970, members of the Weathermen conducted dozens of bombings, including attacks on the Capitol, the Pentagon, and the headquarters of the New York City Police Department. The Weathermen suffered the most serious blow to their organization on March 8, 1970, when three of its leaders died by inadvertently detonating a bomb in a townhouse that served as a bomb factory in New York's Greenwich Village.[40]

Other factors may influence the timing of particular acts of terrorism. The organization may possess a rare opportunity to stage a successful attack or it may have a unique opportunity to strike a target of particularly high value, such as a leading political figure the group opposes. The organization may also believe that, at a particular moment, the cost of an attack is low or that the chances of success are high.[41]

Terrorist organizations may also be influenced by the activities of other groups, a phenomenon known as the "contagion effect of terrorism." The Weathermen, for instance, were heavily influenced by violent insurgencies in Algeria, the Philippines, and Uruguay, suggesting that the roots of terrorism occurring in a particular nation are not explained merely by events in that nation alone, but also by events in other countries.[42] Terrorist

Members of the Weathermen march across a bridge in downtown Chicago, October 11, 1969. At this rally, at least 35 people were arrested for the subsequent window-smashing spree. It was just one instance of violence attributed to the group.

organizations tend to imitate the tactics used by other organizations, if they are believed to have been particularly "successful." The first terrorist hijacking, for instance, was carried out on July 22, 1968, by the PFLP, but the tactic of hijacking was quickly adopted by various other terrorist groups during the late 1960s and 1970s. Suicide bombings are another example of how terrorism tactics can be "contagious." Beginning in the late 1990s, suicide bombings, which had previously occurred mainly in Sri Lanka, Israel, and Lebanon, had spread to places as diverse as Morocco, Saudi Arabia, Croatia, Egypt, Iraq, Russia, and, on 9/11, the United States.

TERRORISM AS ASYMMETRIC WARFARE

Terrorism has often been referred to as asymmetric warfare—a tactic used by a group that is believed to be militarily, politically, or economically weaker than its enemy. In asymmetric warfare, the combatants tend to use those tactics that are to their comparative advantage, enabling them to exploit their enemy's relative weaknesses and real or perceived vulnerabilities. Asymmetric warfare implies that one side is either incapable (usually the weaker side) or unwilling (usually the stronger side) to use its opponent's tactics.[43]

Terrorist organizations are often perceived as the "weaker" side in the conflict and will ordinarily be aware that they cannot defeat their enemy militarily. Instead, a group may attempt to achieve its political goals by breaking their enemy's will to fight. Their methods may include using tactics and weapons in ways that are difficult to prevent or defend against; employing the element of surprise; altering the battle space; attempting to make use of all segments of its society; and targeting large segments of the enemy's population.

In the Israeli–Palestinian conflict, for example, the use of suicide bombings by Palestinian terrorist organizations has been chosen for various tactical reasons. Suicide bombings are inherently difficult to defend against; they carry an element of surprise; and they target the entire Israeli population in an indiscriminate manner.

The asymmetric tactics also include attempts to instill fear in the society of the stronger side. Sheikh Ahmed Yassin, who was the spiritual leader of the radical Islamist group Hamas, stated, "The Israelis . . . will fall to their knees. . . . You can sense the fear in Israel already; they are worried about where and when the next attacks will come. Ultimately, Hamas will win."[44]

TERRORIST ORGANIZATIONS AND COST-BENEFIT ANALYSIS

Ultimately, terrorist organizations can be expected to commit an act of violence if they perceive that the benefit that they may gain by staging the attack will outweigh the cost of the attack. Terrorist organizations hence engage in what is referred to as cost-benefit analysis.

There are a number of costs that a terrorist organization will incur by perpetrating a terrorist attack. First, the organization is likely to provoke the government against which the attack was directed into a fierce response that will either weaken the terrorist group or keep the group so preoccupied with eluding the government that it will have little time to plan additional attacks. In the aftermath of the attacks of September 11, 2001, for instance, the United States responded not only by waging a war on al Qaeda, but also by invading Afghanistan and unseating the Taliban, the rulers of Afghanistan who had provided a safe haven for al Qaeda.

A second cost to the terrorist organization is that it may lose popular support, especially if the constituency that the group purports to represent regards the terrorist attack as excessively brutal. On August 15, 1998, for example, the Catholic, anti-British Real IRA (RIRA) packed 500 pounds of explosives into a car, which it then detonated in a popular shopping district in the town of Omagh in Northern Ireland. Twenty-eight people were killed and hundreds more were injured in what was called the single bloodiest incident in Northern Ireland in three decades. The "Omagh Bombing" produced such an outrage, including from the pro-Irish Catholic community, that the RIRA was temporarily forced to suspend its activities.

What kind of benefits does the terrorist organization believe it will gain by committing a politically motivated act of violence? First, the organization believes that its attack will draw attention to the group's cause, which is usually the case, due largely to the emphasis that the media places on acts of violence. Publicity and recognition are among the primary goals of any terrorist group. As Walter Laqueur once noted, "The media are the terrorist's best friend. The terrorist's act by itself is nothing; publicity is all."[45] That terrorists are indeed craving the "oxygen of publicity," as former British Prime Minister Margaret Thatcher once stated,[46] was dramatically showcased in 1975. In that year, a terrorist cell led by Carlos "the Jackal," one of the most notorious terrorists in history, seized a meeting of the Organization of Petroleum-Exporting Countries (OPEC) in Vienna. Carlos kidnapped the attending oil ministers, but waited until the arrival of television crews before fleeing from the premises along with his hostages.[47]

Terrorists often manage to create a state of extreme fear in the larger population, hoping to bring popular attitudes in line with the terrorist group's own political positions. Terrorist groups also hope to portray their violent actions as heroic deeds. By emphasizing the righteousness of their cause, terrorists ultimately seek not only attention, but also recognition and legitimacy. Finally, the use of TV, radio, the print media, and the Internet are intended to mobilize the terrorists' constituency, increase the recruitment of potential supporters, and raise more funds.[48]

Terrorist organizations also hope to inspire further resistance among similar-minded individuals or groups. Taking the idea of "propaganda by deed" (see Chapter 4) to heart, organizations tend to view violence as a fast track to revolution. Terrorist organizations hope that violence will weaken the government's authority and demoralize the bureaucracy upon which the government's survival depends. Undermining those foundations of the state may then force the government to give in to the group's demands and enable more supporters to join the terrorist group. This rationale lay behind the Cuban Revolution under Fidel Castro. Castro believed that the use of violence would serve as a catalyst to help transform the political situation, eventually ending the dictatorship of Fulgencio Batista. Castro assumed that the violence inflicted by his rebel militia, the so-called People's Army, would excite, awaken, and mobilize the masses. Castro was eventually successful in unseating Batista, though due more to the ineptitude

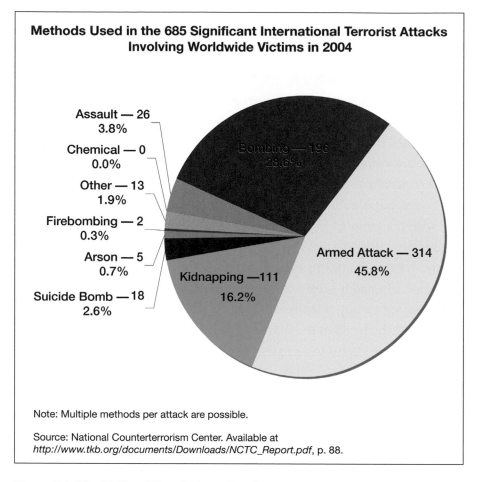

Methods Used in the 685 Significant International Terrorist Attacks Involving Worldwide Victims in 2004

Assault — 26
3.8%

Chemical — 0
0.0%

Other — 13
1.9%

Firebombing — 2
0.3%

Arson — 5
0.7%

Suicide Bomb — 18
2.6%

Kidnapping —111
16.2%

Bombing — 196
28.6%

Armed Attack — 314
45.8%

Note: Multiple methods per attack are possible.

Source: National Counterterrorism Center. Available at
http://www.tkb.org/documents/Downloads/NCTC_Report.pdf, p. 88.

Figure 3.1 The National Counterterrorism Center was created by President George W. Bush to support Central Intelligence in their gathering and analysis of information about terrorism. The pie chart above represents their statistics on methods used in international terrorist attacks in 2004.

of Batista's government and military than because Castro managed to stir up the Cuban masses.

Terrorist organizations may seek to provoke a harsh response by the government against which the attacks are directed. The reason is partly because organizations hope that this might increase sympathy and support for their group's cause. There may also be underlying psychological reasons, whereby groups subconsciously attempt to provoke such a response in order to convince themselves of the righteousness of their own cause. An example is the West-German Red Army Faction (RAF), which repeatedly tried, without success, to show the "true face" of the German leadership, which the RAF labeled fascist. Similarly, Carlos Marighella, the main theorist behind the concept of the "urban guerrilla," wrote that acts of terrorism or insurrection should be aimed at provoking the authorities into a repressive overreaction, which the terrorists can then exploit to their political advantage.

SUMMARY

If we want to understand the roots of terrorism, we must understand not only the individual who carries out the terrorist attack, but also the terrorist organization, its goals, and motives. This chapter examined the rationales by which terrorist organizations may justify violent attacks.

We have seen that terrorist groups strive to maintain themselves, and this "survival instinct" may at times lead the organization to act. Terrorist organizations are also motivated to strike because their guiding ideology may require them to do so.

Terrorism can be construed as the result of an internal decision-making mechanism, whereby the group chooses to conduct an act of terrorism out of a set of possible choices. Sometimes, terrorism will be the "last resort" for a group, after it has tried other tactics. However, the terrorist organization eventually concludes that terrorism serves its cause better than other non-violent methods. Once the organization has reached this conclusion, it will strike at a time that it believes to be opportune.

The terrorist group also believes that the costs of terrorist attacks are outweighed by their benefits. For outsiders, it may seem shocking that groups can rationalize the killing of innocent civilians so that these killings "make sense" to them.

However, if we really want to understand what drives terrorist groups to engage in acts of murder, we should not simply brush off all terrorist actions as the deeds of a gang of lunatics. From the perspective of the terrorist within the organization, killing is not regarded as abhorrent. He will see the violent act as a logical step that will bring him closer to the specific goal that he has set for himself. Terrorist organizations, by making a willful choice that is in line with their goals—however detestable—have an internal logic that we need to understand if we want to reduce the spread of terrorism.

CHAPTER 4

POLITICAL EXPLANATIONS OF TERRORISM

On the morning of September 5, 1972, eight terrorists entered the Olympic Village in Munich, Germany. The men—members of an armed wing of the Palestine Liberation Organization (PLO) calling itself "Black September"—were on their way to the facilities that housed the Israeli athletic team at the 1972 Olympics. At about 4:30 A.M., the men stormed the compound of the Israeli delegation, immediately shot two athletes, and took nine others hostage. Shortly after, they demanded that Israel release 236 jailed Palestinians and that Germany release five members of the Red Army Faction (RAF) in exchange for the Israeli hostages. Should their demands not be met, they threatened to kill an Israeli athlete every two hours.

After 15 hours of negotiations, it was agreed that two helicopters would transport the terrorists and the hostages to the airbase at Fürstenfeldbruck, from where they would fly to Cairo, Egypt, on a Lufthansa aircraft. The West German government, however, did not intend to follow the plan. Instead, it decided to attempt a hostage rescue, a decision that soon turned out to be tragic. Not only did the poorly trained and ill-equipped West German police underestimate the number of terrorists, but Germany did not possess an anti-terror unit trained to handle this kind of situation.

When the two helicopters touched down at the airbase at 10:35 P.M., five West German police sharpshooters opened fire on the terrorists. The exchange of fire was followed by a stand-off between the terrorists and the police, and eventually by a police decision to attack. Shortly after midnight, after several of the hostages had already been shot, one of the terrorists hurled a grenade into one of the helicopters, killing the remaining Israeli athletes. At the end of one of the most shocking days in the history of international terrorism, nine Israeli athletes, one West German policeman, and several terrorists were dead.

Although the Palestinian militants failed to achieve their objective—the release of jailed Palestinians and Germans—they did manage a victory in another respect: The massacre at Munich focused the attention of the world on a larger political issue, the Palestinian cause, which now could no longer be ignored. Like few events before 1972, the Munich massacre showed that despite the brutality and cruelty with which terrorists operated, the use of violence, at times, could bring groups closer to achieving their political goals.

This chapter will examine the political roots of terrorism. "Terrorism . . . is fundamentally and inherently political," writes Dr. Bruce Hoffman, a leading terrorism expert.[49] It is violence, or the threat of violence, "used and directed in pursuit of, or in service of, a political aim." Given that terrorism is a political phenomenon—a type of politically motivated violence—political motives are key to understanding what lies behind the use of terrorism.

The chapter will first provide a historical sketch of the development of political terrorism. We will then examine four different types of political terrorism: ethno-nationalist/separatist, revolutionary/left-wing, right-wing, and state-sponsored terrorism. The chapter will also outline some of the political motivations for why groups may adopt terrorist tactics.

THE ORIGINS OF POLITICAL TERRORISM

Historically, terrorism has come in a variety of shapes and forms. If one defines terrorism to include assassinations,[50] then terrorism dates as far back as the ancient Greek democracies and Roman republics. The murder of Julius Caesar in 44 B.C. by a group of conspiratorial senators, for example, could count as an ancient example of political terrorism. Until the nineteenth century, most movements and groups that employed terrorist tactics were predominantly religious in character, although their actions were at times politically motivated. These groups included the Jewish Zealots and Sicarii (A.D. 66–73), the Muslim Assassins (eleventh–thirteenth century), and the Hindu Thuggee (seventh–nineteenth century), which will be discussed in Chapter 7.

Modern political terrorism, as well as the words *terror* and *terrorism*, dates back to the French Revolution. In 1793, aristocratic elements outside of France conspired with foreign rulers to invade France, thus threatening the revolutionary government. The government also suspected treason within its own borders. On August 30, the Assemblée Nationale, the French legislative convention, which was then led by a radical faction known as the Jacobins, adopted an official policy of *terreur* (terror) in order to suppress the reactionary elements that threatened to reverse the dynamic of the French Revolution and reestablish the old order, known as the *ancien régime.*

Led by Maximilien Robespierre, the Jacobins set out to eliminate the enemies of the revolution. For them, *terreur* was a necessary part of the revolution and would eventually guarantee the triumph of democracy. Thus, in the early years of its use, the word *terror* had a decidedly positive connotation. Yet, the "purification" of the "subversives" took on a life of its own and, soon after the proclamation of the Reign of Terror, more and more people, even those who initially supported the Jacobins, were designated "enemies of the revolution" and treated accordingly. As a result of the Reign of Terror, which lasted from August 30, 1793, until July 27, 1794, 300,000 "subversives" were arrested and 17,000 were officially killed, while many others perished in prison. Most of those killed died by the guillotine, a machine that had been invented a few years earlier as a "humane" method of execution by decapitation.

The *régime de la terreur* soon came to an end as more and more of Robespierre's former supporters met their fate at the guillotine. Unable to accuse him of *terreur* because of their earlier support of this method as a legitimate instrument of government, the conspirators accused Robespierre of *terrorisme* (terrorism), a label that suggested illegal conduct. Robespierre himself was eventually guillotined on July 28, 1794. His execution brought to an abrupt end the Reign of Terror and, with it, the event which would be marked in history as the beginning of modern political terrorism.[51]

The terror of the French Revolution was organized, systematic, and designed to achieve a political goal. In contrast to terrorism as we commonly understand it today, however, the terror of the Jacobins came from the state itself rather than from a group that challenges the state. To be sure, state-based terror was a common feature throughout the twentieth century and has been responsible for countless millions of deaths—many times more than terrorism "from below." Nazi Germany under Adolf Hitler, the Soviet Union under Joseph Stalin, Chile under Augusto Pinochet, Iraq under Saddam Hussein, and various other states have used terror as one method to suppress segments of their population. Nevertheless, we commonly understand terrorism as a tactic used by so-called non-state actors—organizations that exist either within states ("sub-national" or "sub-state actors") or that transcend states ("transnational actors").

What brought about this change in how we understand political terrorism, from a state-based to a non-state-based phenomenon? The answer can be found in the transformations that occurred in the aftermath of the French Revolution. Foremost was the rise of nationalism and the related concepts of nationhood, statehood, citizenship, and shared identities of nationally defined groups of people. These powerful historical transformations gave rise to the modern nation-states of today, such as Germany and Italy. This rise of nationalism was incompatible with the absolutism common in Europe until the nineteenth century, according to which the monarch had a "divine right" to rule. The birth of nationalism led to a rise in anti-monarchic sentiments that eventually manifested themselves in terrorism aimed at the state.

Other important transformations that had an impact on the formation of modern terrorism were socio-economic in nature. The Industrial Revolution, which began in England and then swept through continental Europe during the nineteenth century, had a profound effect on those societies. As more people began to work in large factories, often inhumane conditions resulted in an increasingly disenchanted and alienated populace. One outcome of the deep societal changes during this period was the emergence of modern ideologies such as Marxism, which deplored what it labeled the "exploitation of the proletariat" and advocated the overthrow of capitalism, which was to be replaced by the rule of the working class.

According to Walter Laqueur, "systematic terrorism" began in the second half of the nineteenth century and comprised three general types.[52] The first variety was exemplified by Russian revolutionaries. Most important among them was the

Narodnaya Volya (People's Will), which fought the Russian Tsar's autocratic rule from 1878–1881. The Narodnaya Volya was likely the first organization that adopted the concept of "propaganda by deed." According to "propaganda by deed," theoretical propaganda such as group gatherings, pamphlets, or newspapers was not sufficient to advance a group's goal. Instead, violence, rather than merely words, is necessary to draw attention to the cause and to rally the masses behind the revolution. "Propaganda by deed" has influenced terrorist groups ever since its formulation. The Narodnaya Volya violently resisted the oppressive rule of Tsar Aleksander II, targeting him and his close family members and government circles. Following eight unsuccessful attempts on his life, on March 1, 1881,

Anarchism

Mahatma Gandhi (1869–1948) is mostly remembered for helping to bring about India's independence from British rule through non-violent protest. Few, however, would think of the Indian leader as one of the most prominent examples of an anarchist—testimony to a common misunderstanding about the concept of anarchism. Anarchism is a doctrine that opposes established political authority in all its forms. Anarchists view the state as an oppressor that uses various institutions of coercion—the army, police, bureaucracy, and the courts—to maintain tight control over the individual, thus limiting his freedom.

Benign anarchists such as Gandhi or "Prince" Peter Kropotkin believed that mutual aid and cooperation, not conflict, are the basic laws of societies. They were convinced of the innate goodness of human beings and did not promote violence as a mechanism for social change.

Influenced by worsening labor conditions during the Industrial Revolution in the nineteenth century, other branches of anarchism openly espoused violence by adopting the concept of "propaganda by deed." Mikhail Bakunin (1814–1876) and Sergey Nechayev (1847–1882), the Russian revolutionaries succeeded in killing the Tsar by detonating a bomb in the streets of St. Petersburg as he drove by. Although the Tsarist secret police managed to crack down on the Narodnaya Volya a short time after the assassination, the group left a lasting impression on subsequent revolutionaries, including anarchist groups in Spain, Italy, France, and the United States.

Anarchism is the second variety of political terrorism that emerged in the nineteenth century. Although anarchist groups suffered from poor organization, their emphasis on individual action resulted in sporadic successes, including the 1901 assassination of U.S. President William McKinley by an unaffiliated anarchist.

two Russian revolutionary agitators, were among the main theorists of a variant of anarchism that regarded violence as a tactical necessity. The aim of the protest movement fathered by Bakunin was to crush capitalism and democracy (which was identified with the bourgeoisie) and shake society to its very foundations. Anarchists did not develop elaborate political theories, believing that once the bourgeoisie is crushed, peace will follow naturally.

After the 1870s, anarchist terrorism began to spread from Europe to the United States, where anarchist workers, encouraged by the availability of dynamite, were responsible for a series of bombings. By the late 1920s, anarchist terrorism had passed its peak. A lack of organization in the anarchist movement and an inherent lack of patience, characteristic of many anarchists, were responsible for the failure of anarchism to effect political change.

Despite its failure to impact politics, the violent anarchism of Bakunin influenced the thinking of subsequent generations of terrorists. In the United States, anarchist theories have also been highly appealing to intellectuals, students, and youth in general, especially in the protest against the Vietnam War during the 1960s and 1970s.

The third variety of political terrorism that emerged in the nineteenth century largely as a response to the forces of nationalism were radical nationalist groups striving for political autonomy or national independence. These included Armenian, Macedonian, Irish, Polish, Serb, and Indian terrorist groups, among many others.

Until World War I, terrorism was regarded as a predominantly left-wing phenomenon. In the inter-war period (1918–1939) and until the end of World War II in 1945, most terrorist operations were perpetrated by right-wing and nationalist-separatist groups, such as the fascist Croatian Ustasha, which fought for an independent Croatian state. At the same time, terror during those years was identified largely with the brutal repression characteristic of totalitarian states such as fascist Italy, Nazi Germany, and the Stalinist Soviet Union. Terror became intimately intertwined with Nazi and fascist rule, often assuming the status of semi-official state policy. The adoption of official state terror created "a system of government-sanctioned fear and coercion" ensuring "complete and submissive compliance" through the suppression of the declared enemies of the state, including Jews and communists.[53]

After World War II and until the 1970s, the emphasis of international political terrorism was again revolutionary. In the first two decades after the war, nationalist and anti-colonialist groups resisted European foreign rule in Asia, the Middle East, and Africa. Those who sympathized with the terrorists, who now struggled for self-determination, often labeled them "freedom fighters."

In the 1960s and 1970s, the anti-colonialist struggle subsided as more countries gained their independence, but terrorism remained revolutionary in character. There were nationalist and ethnic separatist groups such as the Irish Republican Army, the Basque ETA, and the Palestine Liberation Organization (PLO) that continued their struggle for self-determination. The 1960s and 1970s also witnessed the rise of left-wing extremism drawn in large part from radical student organizations in Western Europe, Latin America, and the United States. The extremism of the radical "new left" rested on Marxist, Leninist, Maoist, and Trotskyite ideology and was heavily influenced by the Vietnam War, which was seen as the latest aggression of a Western capitalist-military-industrial conspiracy.

While the revolutionary connotation continues today, terrorism in the 1990s and at the beginning of the twenty-first century has become a more complex phenomenon. There has been a growing connection between political terrorism and organized crime. Also, the 1990s saw a growing trend of state-sponsored terrorism, with countries such as Libya, Iraq, Iran, Sudan, and Syria featured on the U.S. State Department's list of state sponsors of terrorism. Finally, since the mid 1990s, religiously motivated terrorism has become the most dominant and most dangerous variety. A series of high-profile attacks by religious terrorist groups, one of which included the use of nerve gas, raised the specter of mass destruction inflicted by groups with the capabilities and intention to harm their enemies. The increase in use of highly lethal tactics, such as suicide bombings, and the strengthening of an uncompromising radical version of Islamist thought, combined with the spread of weapons of mass destruction, have raised the threat potential posed by terrorism. The more dangerous form of terrorism that has emerged has been dubbed the "New Terrorism" because it consists of "different motives, different actors, different sponsors, and . . . demonstrably greater lethality." [54]

TYPES OF POLITICAL TERRORISM

Today, we distinguish among several types of terrorism: ethno-nationalist/separatist, revolutionary/left-wing, right-wing, state-sponsored, and religious terrorism. Religious terrorism, which has become the predominant contemporary threat, will be treated separately in Chapter 7.

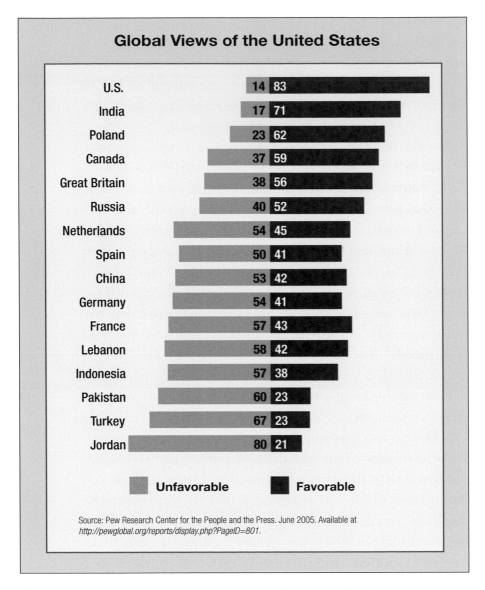

Global Views of the United States

Country	Unfavorable	Favorable
U.S.	14	83
India	17	71
Poland	23	62
Canada	37	59
Great Britain	38	56
Russia	40	52
Netherlands	54	45
Spain	50	41
China	53	42
Germany	54	41
France	57	43
Lebanon	58	42
Indonesia	57	38
Pakistan	60	23
Turkey	67	23
Jordan	80	21

■ Unfavorable   ■ Favorable

Source: Pew Research Center for the People and the Press. June 2005. Available at
http://pewglobal.org/reports/display.php?PageID=801.

Figure 4.1 The Pew Research Center for the People and the Press have made a survey of "global attitudes" one of their main projects. This graph shows the results from their interviews of people in 50 countries, as of June 2005.

The categorization presented here is not the only way in which terrorism can be classified, and there is no agreement among terrorism analysts about any single "typology" of terrorism.

Neither are these categories mutually exclusive, and in fact many terrorist groups can be placed in several categories at once. The Irish Republican Army, for example, is ordinarily understood as an ethno-nationalist/separatist organization, but its doctrine also contains revolutionary and left-wing thought.

Ethno-Nationalist/Separatist Terrorism

Groups in this category use violence in the hope that it will help them establish a state for their own ethnic or national community. They are sometimes called separatist groups, especially if they are attached to a certain territory that they regard as their national homeland. They ordinarily seek the secession of that territory from the state at which their violence is directed. One example of a separatist terrorist organization is the Basque Homeland and Freedom (ETA), a group that fights for self-determination of the Basque people in an independent Basque homeland (Euskadi) in the region bordering Spain and France. The Basques are a Christian group whose own language and culture distinguishes them from both Spaniards and the French. ETA was formed in 1959 in response to Spanish dictator Francisco Franco's attempts to suppress the Basque language and culture. It has staged both high-profile attacks on Spanish officials and government buildings and lower-profile attacks on regional officials and institutions, journalists, and civilians.

In the Middle East, nationalist terrorist groups include the Irgun (Etzel) and Lehi, two Jewish terrorist groups that fought to oust the British from Palestine and establish an independent Jewish state of Israel; the PLO, which aimed its terrorism at Israel, seeking to create a Palestinian state; and the Algerian National Liberation Front, which opposed French rule in Algeria during the 1950s. The Kurdistan Workers Party (PKK) seeks to create an independent Kurdish state in southeastern Turkey and parts of neighboring states with sizable Kurdish populations. The roughly 25 million Kurds are a predominantly Sunni Muslim ethnic community with a culture and language of its own. Kurdistan, the mountainous region populated by the Kurds, includes southeastern Turkey, parts of northern Iraq, western Iran, and regions in Syria and Armenia. Founded in 1973, the PKK is known mostly for attacks on Turkish security forces as well as Turkish targets in several Western European countries. The PKK's leader, Abdullah Ocalan, was arrested by Turkish security forces in February 1999.

Perhaps the best-known ethno-nationalist terrorist group of the twentieth century was the Irish Republican Army (IRA). The IRA formally renounced terrorism in 2005, though various splinter groups of the IRA continue to use terrorist methods.

Revolutionary/Left-Wing Terrorism

Revolutionary terrorism dates back to the Narodnaya Volya (described previously) and is heavily influenced by Marxist and other socialist and communist thought. Revolutionary left-wing terrorist organizations were common in Western Europe and the United States from the late 1960s to early 1980s. Their violence is usually directed against their own governments, which these groups perceive as authoritarian and fascist. They lament the capitalist nature of these regimes and accuse them of exploiting their populations. Idealism, pacifism, anti-imperialism, and an overall belief of the corruption of leadership and society are integral to revolutionary/left-wing ideology.

Two prominent revolutionary/left-wing terrorist organizations, the Weathermen and Symbionese Liberation Army, have been active in the United States. The case of the Weathermen shows the profound effect of the Vietnam War on revolutionary left-wing terrorism. The group's activity had a spillover effect on Western Europe, where two of the most important revolutionary terrorist organizations, the Red Army Faction (RAF) and the Red Brigades, were active in Germany and Italy, respectively. Officially formed in May 1970, the RAF proclaimed itself the enemy of what it believed was a fascist German government. It adopted elements of anarchism and believed violence to be the best way to bring about a socialist society in Germany. The RAF staged a number of bombing attacks in Germany against pro-government publishing houses, department stores, and U.S. army bases. It was also notorious for its attacks and kidnappings of high-profile German personalities such as judges and bankers.[55]

Unlike the RAF in Germany, the Red Brigades posed a serious threat to the survival of the democratic state in Italy. As in Germany, the terrorism of the Red Brigades developed out of student protests. The Red Brigades was formed in Milan, where several militant members of the student movements had been killed during police attacks and brawls with right-wing militants. The Red Brigades' ideology was Marxist-Leninist. It claimed to represent the working class and declared the capitalist system, spearheaded by the "fascist" Christian Democratic party, as their enemy. Many of its attacks were concentrated on factories, but politicians were also targeted. In 1978, the Red Brigades kidnapped Prime Minister Aldo Moro and killed him after 55 days of detention. Other targets of the Red Brigades included real estate, supermarkets, small businesses, drug dealers, and security guards.[56]

Right-Wing Terrorism

The modern phenomenon of right-wing terrorism is often neglected in the terrorism literature because right-wing violence tends to be poorly organized, and because there are few readily identifiable right-wing terrorist organizations. The modern right-wing variant of political terrorism is mainly a European phenomenon that appeared in Western Europe beginning in the 1980s and in Eastern European countries in the late 1980s and 1990s, following the collapse of the former Soviet Union.

Groups associated with right-wing terrorism include neo-Nazi and neo-fascist skinhead gangs that target immigrants and refugees. They are both racist and anti-Semitic and call openly for the demise of democratic states and their replacement with totalitarian states based on the model of fascist Italy or Nazi Germany. They attack the democratic state for its diversity of opinions, social welfare policies, and relatively lax asylum and immigration laws. The core of this movement, which includes skinheads, right-wing hooligans, youth sympathizers, and intellectual guides, believes that only when the state is able to rid itself of the foreign elements that undermine it from within can the state provide for its rightful, natural citizens.

Although modern right-wing activists revere Italian and German fascism, and echo slogans developed by nineteenth-century and early twentieth-century nationalist theorists such as Count Joseph Arthur de Gobineau, Houston Stewart Chamberlain, and Heinrich von Treitschke, modern neo-Nazis and neo-fascists often lack a rigorous ideological belief system. The phenomenon of right-wing terrorism appears to be in part a manifestation of widespread youth disillusionment and "egocentric pleasure derived from brawling and bombing."[57] This is, of course, not to minimize the grave danger that modern right-wing activism poses both to those elements of society that it considers inferior as well as to democratic systems.

State-Sponsored Terrorism

Governments have long engaged in the systematic use of terror against foreign and domestic enemies. From 1933 to 1945, Nazi Germany terrorized and killed millions of Jews, communists, homosexuals, Gypsies, the mentally and physically disabled, and other persons it regarded as "subhuman." Such official, state-based policies are commonly referred to as "terror" and are thus distinguished from terrorism, which is usually understood as violence emanating from non-state actors. In contrast to the terror that states have wreaked on their own populations, modern state-sponsored terrorism, as it developed beginning in the 1980s, has been deliberately embraced by certain nations as an extension and integral part of their foreign policy. It has enabled them to wage relatively low-cost covert and proxy wars on their enemies by using surrogate organizations and groups.[58]

In 2005, the U.S. State Department listed five countries— Cuba, Libya, North Korea, Sudan, and Syria—as state sponsors of terrorism. In October 2004, the United States had removed Iraq from this list. Iraq, under the leadership of former dictator Saddam Hussein, had been listed as a state sponsor for the previous 14 years.

Modern state-sponsored terrorism came into existence during the Iranian Revolution in 1979, when Iranian students, instigated by the revolutionary leader Ayatollah Ruhollah Khomeini, seized the U.S. embassy in Tehran and held over 50 Americans hostage for 444 days. For Iran, and subsequently for other state sponsors of terrorism, supporting terrorist groups was a cheap and relatively low-risk method of using proxies to attack stronger or distant enemies. For terrorist groups that enjoy state sponsorship, support by the state dramatically increases the funding of the group, which in turn enables it to purchase weapons and materiel.

The 2003 issue of the U.S. State Department's annual report "Patterns of Global Terrorism" described Iran as the "most active state sponsor of terrorism in 2003." One of the organizations sponsored by Iran is Hizbollah (Party of God), a radical Islamic organization active in Lebanon that seeks to establish a fundamentalist Islamic state. A fervent opponent of Israel, Hizbollah, which is among the most technically sophisticated terrorist organizations in the world, was established in 1982. The group's prolonged and successful guerrilla campaign against the Israel Defense Forces helped precipitate Israel's withdrawal from Lebanon in 2000. The group continues to pose a threat to the Jewish state through cooperation with various Palestinian terrorist groups active in the West Bank and Gaza Strip.[59] Hizbollah also enjoys the support of another state sponsor of terrorism, Syria, which has served as a transfer station for Iranian supplies to Hizbollah in Lebanon.

A Palestinian taxi driver argues here with an Israeli soldier preventing him from passing through a checkpoint outside of Ramallah. This type of confrontation is often cited as one of the grievances of Palestinians living in Israeli-occupied territory.

POLITICAL MOTIVATIONS FOR TERRORISM

Terrorist groups may be motivated by a wish to seize power or to increase their influence or the influence of the community that it purports to represent. They can also be influenced by a variety of grievances and motivated by a desire to improve political, social, or economic conditions. The political griev-ances that can affect a group's decision to use terrorism include government repression, foreign occupation, and the lack of political freedom. These grievances tend to create feelings of humiliation, which in turn weaken the belief in the righteous-ness of the government. Ideology plays a role in formulating the grievances and suggesting a remedy.

Power and Influence

Power has long been recognized as the central issue of politics in general[60] and it is fundamental to our understanding of terrorism. Terrorism is "ineluctably about power: the pursuit of power, the acquisition of power, and the use of power to achieve political change," writes Bruce Hoffman.[61] During the French Revolution's Reign of Terror and in other instances of state-based oppression, terror was often designed to maintain the state's power by suppressing the so-called enemies of the state. Terrorist organizations are motivated not only by the desire to acquire political influence, but also to weaken that of their enemies. They do not always have a workable plan to unseat the government to which they are opposed, and their political objectives are often ill-defined. Nevertheless, the allure of power and influence is what leads to the formation of many terrorist organizations, and it is what keeps the organization motivated.

Grievances: Repression, Occupation, and Humiliation

Political, social, and economic discontent is perhaps as important as power and influence in explaining the political causes of terrorism. In the aftermath of September 11, a number of factors were believed to have contributed to the hatred of the United States and the terrorist attacks against America. One factor was the widespread discontent of Arabs and Muslims about U.S. foreign policy vis-à-vis the Middle East. The list of grievances included historical Western colonization of Arab states and holy Muslim territory; American support for Israel and some Arab regimes deemed repressive; the exploitation of natural resources, most importantly oil; and the poverty of Middle Easterners linked to Western exploitation. The argument was that U.S. policy infuriated and humiliated Arabs and Muslims, and led a tiny, yet extremely radical fringe to adopt terrorist tactics.

Several common grievances have given rise to terrorism throughout history. Prominent among those is the occupation of territory by a foreign power. One of the best-known examples of the use of terrorism to end foreign rule took place in Algeria between 1954 and 1962. The struggle of Algerian nationalists against French rule, led by the Algerian National Liberation Front (FLN), remains a classic case of anti-colonial rebellion. In 1956, the FLN began attacking French targets in Algiers, after previously focusing its struggle on the countryside. Using female fighters, the FLN targeted mainly bars and cafes frequented by the French colonialists, the so-called *pied-noir*. It also embarked on a series of assassinations that culminated in the killing of the mayor of Algiers. By 1957, the French army was put in charge of controlling the unruly situation. It clamped down with a heavy hand not only against members of the FLN, but also against many suspected terrorists who were in fact innocent. Torture became common, and soon both the Algerian and French publics were appalled at the brutal methods used by the French forces. While the tough French policy resulted in the defeat of the FLN, the latter nevertheless managed to focus attention on the situation in Algeria. French rule came to an end in 1962, and Algeria was declared an independent country.

Israel's occupation of the West Bank and the Gaza Strip, territory populated by Palestinians, is perhaps the best contemporary example of the link between occupation and terrorism. Since the occupation began in 1967, Israel has established a stubborn civil administration in these territories to strengthen its control, leaving the Palestinian population in these areas frustrated, humiliated, and angry. The civil administration, along with its sometimes hostile officials, have left a permanent blemish on Israeli-Palestinian relations.[62]

Israeli roadblocks and army checkpoints that hamper Palestinians' free movement have prompted additional resentment among the Palestinian population. After interviewing Palestinian prisoners on the effects of the occupation, Israeli journalists recounted their grievances: "All complained of the insult and humiliation repeatedly suffered at army roadblocks and checkpoints: the nasty tone in which they were addressed, the body searches accompanied by shoves and shouts, the derision they were forced to endure in front of family and friends." [63] The Algerian and Palestinian cases show that foreign rule, which often entails the denial of political freedoms and national self-determination for the occupied people, can produce conditions that give rise to terrorism.

Terrorism, however, is not necessarily the product of foreign rule. Historically, terrorism has also emerged and intensified as a tactic against homegrown authoritarianism and government repression. The Russian Tsar's brutal response to the populist movement in the second half of the nineteenth century was a factor in the development of the Narodnaya Volya. [64] One reason why severe government repression can lead to terrorist violence is the desire for revenge that it will provoke. According to Dr. Martha Crenshaw, "If there is a single common emotion that drives the individual to become a terrorist, it is vengeance on behalf of comrades or even the constituency the terrorist aspires to represent . . . A regime thus encourages terrorism when it creates martyrs to be avenged. Anger at what is perceived as unjust persecution inspires demands for revenge, and as the regime responds to terrorism with greater force, violence escalates out of control." [65]

Terrorism has also emerged as a tactic against the most extreme form of authoritarianism—totalitarianism. During World War II, the Nazi dictatorship produced a number of partisan movements that resisted Nazi occupation both within Germany and in its conquered territories. Terrorism as a response to totalitarian rule, however, has not proven very successful. Unlike democracies, totalitarian states have no inhibitions on using brute force to crush any opposition. [66]

Terrorism is often successful in so-called weak states, however. Weak states are defined as those that see an abundance of armed challengers to the central authority; where the government has difficulty controlling parts of its territory; and where the government has difficulty providing for basic services. [67]

Political, social, and economic grievances in a society raise the likelihood of terrorism. Such grievances are often the result of government oppression and the denial of political freedom. Foreign rule and domination have a particularly strong effect and lead to widespread feelings of humiliation and frustration among large segments of a population, which may be more prone to use violent tactics in order to change the situation.

But grievances alone do not explain the emergence of terrorism in all situations and it is unclear why some societies react to certain grievances by producing terrorist organizations when other societies do not. In addition, terrorism has occurred in countries where there are relatively few grievances, such as Western Europe or the United States. We must therefore conclude that there is no objective standard by which we could measure when a grievance produces terrorism. The same disaffection that may lead to terrorism in one place may not lead to violent resistance in another. In thinking about grievances as a cause of terrorism, it is more useful to look at how societies and groups perceive grievances than to analyze the actual degree of discontent.

The Role of Ideology

Political explanations of terrorism are closely linked to ideologies. Ideology is defined as a system of beliefs and values; examples include communism, nationalism, or Islamism. Ideology helps terrorist organizations rationalize and justify the use of violence in a number of different ways. A particular ideology might criticize the existing order as inhumane and immoral, thus undermining the regime in power. A common ideology gives revolutionaries and terrorists a sense of unity and solidarity, and helps such a group mobilize recruits. Ideologies help define how groups view the world and how they identify their enemies. Using an ideology, such as communism, helps a terrorist group displace responsibility for its actions on its enemies, who become "deserving" of their treatment.[68]

While most terrorist groups espouse some form of ideology, their commitment to it is often weak.[69] Groups have, at times, shifted ideologies or combined ideologies. Both the IRA and ETA, for instance, have shifted their ideological orientations from nationalism to socialism, and now each group seems to have combined the two. The Palestinian Hamas combines a religious and a nationalist ideology.

The case of Hizbollah illuminates how adaptable ideologies can be. In 1982, when Hizbollah adopted the tactic of suicide bombings, it was undeterred by the fact that Islam strictly forbids Muslims to commit suicide. Religious scholars associated with Hizbollah simply reinterpreted religious doctrine to make it fit with the group's tactical needs.

SUMMARY

Political terrorism has many facets. Terror during the French Revolution, which was state-based and seen as a virtue, was an entirely different concept from the subsequent revolutionary and nationalistic terrorism directed at the state. There are several different types of terrorism—ethno-nationalist/separatist, revolutionary/left-wing, right-wing, and state-sponsored terrorism—although they are not mutually exclusive, and many contemporary terrorist groups belong to more than one of these categories.

What these different types of terrorism have in common is that their nature and aims are political. Terrorist organizations want to increase their influence and power, regardless of how unrealistic their ambitions are. Political conditions that give rise to terrorist groups include grievances that may be the result of foreign rule and occupation or repression by a home-grown authoritarian government. The denial of basic rights and participation in politics does not lead to terrorism in every single case, but it is certain to humiliate and frustrate those at the receiving end of such treatment. The role of ideology is to provide the terrorist organization with a sense of direction and the justification to use violence.

CHAPTER 5

THE ROLE OF ECONOMICS, MODERNIZATION, AND GLOBALIZATION

Shortly after the terrorist attacks of 9/11, President George W. Bush deliberated over a response to the wanton killings on U.S. soil. Ultimately, he declared a "war on terrorism," a challenge he described as a "struggle against hateful groups that exploit poverty and despair."[70] The belief that terrorism has economic causes is widespread. As the South Korean President Kim Dae-jung, who won the Nobel Peace Prize in 2000, has noted, "at the bottom of terrorism is poverty. That is the main cause. Then there are other religious, national, and ideological differences."[71] Desmond Tutu, a South African Bishop and 1984 Nobel Peace prize laureate, once said that "external circumstances such as poverty and a sense of grievance and injustice can fill people with resentment and despair to the point of desperation."[72]

This chapter will look at the relationship between economic factors and terrorism, and specifically whether terrorism is caused by poverty. It will show that terrorism is sometimes motivated by greed rather than by grievances. The remainder of the chapter will examine the role modernization and globalization play with regard to the occurrence and persistence of terrorism.

THE ECONOMIC ROOTS OF TERRORISM

There is a widespread belief that terrorism is caused, at least in part, by economic distress. Poverty, the argument goes, frustrates people. Over time, their frustration turns into outright aggression against those believed to be responsible for their plight. Much social scientific research, however, has challenged the conventional wisdom that terrorism is the direct result of poverty or poor education.

An extensive study published in 1983, for example, found that most people involved in terrorist activities were well educated. Roughly two-thirds of identified members of terrorist groups had some university training, graduated from universities, or were active postgraduate students. Moreover, approximately the same percentage came from the middle or upper classes.[73]

More recent research has shown that "in the forty-nine countries currently designated by the United Nations as the least developed hardly any terrorist activity occurs."[74]

A poll conducted of more than 1,000 Palestinians showed little evidence that more highly educated Palestinians were less supportive of violent resistance against Israel.[75] Unemployed Palestinians were found to be less supportive of armed attacks against Israeli military, and especially civilian, targets. If poverty were to blame for the broad support for terrorism among Palestinians,[76] one would expect that the unemployed individuals—those at the bottom of the economic ladder—would strongly advocate violence against Israelis, who are commonly thought to be responsible for the Palestinians' circumstances.

25 LEAST DEVELOPED COUNTRIES

1.	Afghanistan
2.	Angola
3.	Bangladesh
4.	Benin
5.	Bhutan
6.	Burkina Faso
7.	Burundi
8.	Cambodia
9.	Cape Verde
10.	Central African Republic
11.	Chad
12.	Comoros
13.	Democratic Republic of the Congo
14.	Djibouti
15.	Equatorial Guinea
16.	Eritrea
17.	Ethiopia
18.	Gambia
19.	Guinea
20.	Guinea-Bissau
21.	Haiti
22.	Kiribati
23.	Lao People's Democratic Republic
24.	Lesotho
25.	Liberia

Source: United Nations Conference on Trade and Development. Available at
http://www.unctad.org/Templates/WebFlyer.asp?intItemID=3432&lang=1.

Table 5.1 This table lists the 25 least-developed countries in the world, according to the United Nations Conference on Trade and Development. While there is a widespread belief that terrorism may be caused by economic distress, the link between poverty and terrorism is neither simple nor direct.

There is additional evidence suggesting that the relationship between poverty and terrorism is more complex than often assumed. In Lebanon, for instance, the poverty rate among members of Hizbollah—a group designated as a Foreign Terrorist Organization by the U.S. State Department—was lower than the poverty rate among the Lebanese population at large. In addition, Hizbollah fighters were more highly educated. Similarly, extremists from a Jewish terrorist group known as the Jewish Underground (Makhteret), a group responsible for several attacks between 1980 and 1984 that killed a total of 23 Palestinians and injured 191 others, were found to be mostly well educated with high-paying occupations. This suggests that the connection between poverty, education, and terrorism is indirect and weak.[77]

One explanation is that terrorist organizations tend to avoid recruiting the extremely poor, for a simple reason: Terrorists from a middle- or upper-class background are better suited to adjust to a foreign environment, something that a particular mission will often require. To conduct the 9/11 attacks, for example, al Qaeda placed a terrorist cell in the German city of Hamburg. Mohammed Atta, Marwan al-Shehi, Ziad Jarrah, and other would-be hijackers lived in Germany for several years and appeared to adjust to the Western way of life with an ease that might have been difficult for a member of the lower class. As terrorism expert Michael Radu put it, "Al Qaeda has no use for illiterate peasants. They cannot participate in World Trade Center–like attacks, unable as they are to make themselves inconspicuous in the West and lacking the education and training terrorist operatives need."[78] Terrorism is predominantly used by privileged classes. The poorer elements of society may constitute the social base of support for terrorist groups, but they lack the financial and political resources necessary to assume leadership roles in terrorist activity.

Although poverty is not a direct cause of terrorism, it would be improper to conclude that poverty has no effect on terrorism at all. Poverty is very likely to have a number of indirect effects. First, poor countries often serve as safe havens for terrorist groups for various reasons. These countries might be failed states, their governments unable to exercise control over some or all of their territory. Terrorists in these places may be allowed to roam freely. In other situations, poor countries harbor terrorist organizations because they are able to reap financial rewards. Two of the poorest countries in the world, Afghanistan and Sudan, have in the past provided shelter to Osama bin Laden and his al Qaeda movement in return for monetary or military benefits. The Sudanese, for instance, agreed to provide a safe haven for al Qaeda if the latter would assist Sudan in its fight against African Christians in the south and build a number of urgently needed roads.[79]

A second way in which poverty can indirectly affect the occurrence of terrorism is through civil wars. Countries with poor economic conditions are more likely to undergo ethnic and religious conflict, or civil war.[80] In times of economic crisis, the poor are more likely to become involved in crime, riots, and other violent activities.[81] Countries in a civil war, in turn, can either breed homegrown terrorism or attract foreign terrorist elements. Lebanon, Afghanistan, and Sudan are all examples in which civil war provided a hospitable environment for international terrorists to operate.

Finally, poverty makes it easier for the usually more well-to-do leaders of terrorist organizations to exploit the real grievances of the economically disadvantaged masses. While it is true that some terrorist organizations, including various left-wing and ethno-separatist groups, have claimed to act for the sake of the poor and disadvantaged, groups like al Qaeda have not placed poverty at the top of their agenda. They have, however, proven masterful at taking advantage of the real hardships that many people in the Middle East, North Africa, and parts of Asia face—including poverty, income inequalities, and low-quality education.

This 1992 photograph shows two Somali boys suffering from the famine that afflicted their country. Civil war broke out in Somalia, one of the poorest countries in the world, in the 1980s. Such poverty and civil unrest make it easy for terrorist groups to find safe haven in countries like Somalia.

The Arab and Muslim world, where many contemporary terrorist groups originated, suffers from a number of economic deficiencies—lack of productivity; dependence on foreign countries for extraction of raw materials; a focus on the production of primary commodities, rendering technological and information technology know-how irrelevant; lack of economic competition—all of which result in low levels of economic growth. As the Arab Human Development Report stated, "despite the popular perception that Arab countries are rich, the volume of economic product in the region is rather small," only slightly exceeding that of Spain.[82] Whether terrorists are genuinely concerned about the needs of the impoverished and despondent masses is difficult to ascertain. Their willingness and ability to put the anger of the masses to their own use, however, is beyond doubt.

THE BUSINESS OF TERRORISM

There is evidence that for some groups and individuals, financial incentives to participate in terrorist attacks are a part of a complex mix of motivations. Paul Collier, a professor of economics at Oxford University, believes that "civil wars occur where rebel organizations are financially viable."[83] Collier examined the Revolutionary Armed Forces of Columbia (FARC), a group designated by the U.S. State Department as a Foreign Terrorist Organization. Established in 1964, the FARC is the oldest, largest, most capable, and best-equipped insurgency of Marxist origin in Latin America.[84] The FARC's estimated 9,000–12,000 fighters are organized along military lines, and the organization is best described as a militia. In 2003, the group killed over 30 persons and wounded 160 in the car-bombing of a Bogota nightclub. In November 2003, it staged a grenade attack in Bogota's restaurant district, wounding three Americans, and a year later it was involved in a foiled plot to assassinate visiting U.S. president George W. Bush.

The FARC has been able to employ a large number of fighters because of its high revenues—from drug sales and kidnappings—

that amount to around $700 million per year. Collier and other economists view rebellions as the ultimate manifestation of organized crime rather than as protest movements. "Regardless of why the organization is fighting," he argues, "it can only fight if it is financially viable during the conflict."[85]

Dr. Jessica Stern of Harvard University argues not only that terrorist organizations may function as a business, but also that individual members often participate in violent activities in return for financial rewards. Through interviewing leaders and members of terrorist organizations in Pakistan and Kashmir, Dr. Stern found that the reasons that terrorists and militants remain in organizations can shift from what were initially real or perceived grievances or ideological motives, to considerations such as greed, power, attention, or an aspiration to assume leadership of a group. Several high-ranking leaders of terrorist groups conceded that they joined the struggle against their enemies for religious reasons, but that, over time, the salaries they earned have become more important for them.[86] One militant told Dr. Stern that he is making far more money as a fighter for a jihadi organization—a group claiming to fight a holy war—than he would in the civilian sector. Another militant said that initially he believed that his organization was "doing jihad, but now I believe that it is a business and people are earning wealth through it. . . . The public posture is that we are doing jihad in Kashmir," he said, referring to a disputed region bordering India and Pakistan where terrorist organizations are active, "while the real thing is that it is a business empire." He admitted, "First I was there for jihad, now I am there for my financial reasons."[87]

Financial incentives may at least partly motivate Palestinian suicide bombers to volunteer for so-called "martyrdom operations." During the Palestinian "Al Aqsa Intifada," for example, families of suicide bombers usually received cash payments of at least $1,000 from the Palestinian Authority, and $10,000 from the Iraqi government under Saddam Hussein.[88] In March 2002, after Iraq decided to increase the payment to families of suicide bombers from $10,000 to $25,000, there was a steep rise in the number of suicide bombings, suggesting that some Palestinians were seizing a financial opportunity that would leave their families better off.[89]

MODERNIZATION AND ITS EFFECTS ON TERRORISM

Poverty, we have seen, has an indirect rather than a direct effect on people's decision to pursue terrorism. It is also interesting to examine the effect of modernization on terrorism, and in particular whether or not modernization can be considered a cause of terrorism.

Researchers and social scientists are divided over this question. Some scholars believe that modernization has a negative

Terrorism and Organized Crime

Terrorism and organized crime have been traditionally distinguished from one another in terms of their purposes and motivations. While the terrorist strives to attain a political goal and seeks to influence a larger audience to that end, criminals act primarily out of selfish, economic motivations. While the terrorist's primary motivation is political, the criminal's motive is greed.

In recent years, however, there has been a growing trend for criminal organizations and terrorist or guerrilla groups to forge strategic alliances with each other. The new threats posed by these alliances are intensified by the new technologies that allow these entities to endanger Western information systems, a threat known as "cyberterrorism." It has been argued that these trends have expanded the concept of terrorism, whereby these new entities, so-called "non-state actors," pose a significant threat to nation-states.

Two regions where the ties between terrorist and criminal organizations seem particularly strong are Latin America and the former Soviet republics. The Revolutionary Armed Forces of Colombia (FARC) and Peru's Sendero Luminoso (Shining Path), for instance, have provided security support for the production and trafficking

effect on society by weakening the legitimacy of states, thus promoting conflict in general, and the use of political violence,
including terrorism, in particular. Some argue that modernization polarizes society into modernizers and traditionalists. This
argument is related to the concept of "relative deprivation" (RD),
which will be discussed in the next chapter. RD is a theory
according to which wide gaps between people's economic and
political expectations and their actual ability to achieve these
goals leads to their participation in violence. Since modernization takes place rapidly, it has even more detrimental effects
on social stability, dramatically widening the gaps between
individuals' aspirations and their means of achieving their
dreams, and in a shorter time.[90] Rapid economic growth is

of narcotics in Latin America. In Eastern Europe and Central Asia,
close links between terrorist groups and criminal organizations
have increasingly blurred the distinction between the two.

Terrorist groups at times engage in criminal activity in order to
finance their operations. The Provisional IRA, for instance, was
allegedly responsible for a $50 million bank robbery in Northern
Ireland in 2004. Terrorist organizations are also increasingly involved
in the drug trade, a phenomenon known as "narcoterrorism." Drug
trade and trafficking is an extremely lucrative business that helps
terrorist organizations pay for weapons, training, technological
equipment, safe houses, bribes, and other operational needs.
Besides the FARC and the Shining Path, there are many other
terrorist groups that participate in drug trafficking, including
Hizbollah, the Real IRA, the Basque ETA, and the Kurdistan Workers
Party (PKK).

It is very unlikely that organized crime and international terrorism will converge into a single phenomenon. While some terrorists
have been shown to be partly motivated by the possibility of
personal gain, the purpose of terrorism is likely to remain, first and
foremost, political.

Former Iraqi president Saddam Hussein is shown giving a speech in this photograph from 2002. While in power, Hussein paid upwards of $10,000 to the families of Palestinians who committed suicide bombings in Israel.

believed to dissolve existing social norms and structures, while alienating individuals from their social bonds. Individuals in such situations, the theory suggests, become frustrated and drift into terrorist activity.

The optimistic view is that modernization leads to prosperity and political development. Modernization is thought to generate social conditions that will eventually lead to political stability and reduce the likelihood of conflict. Those who subscribe to this view generally are advocates of free trade and open economies, which they believe will lead to democratic rule.

The debate on modernization is unlikely to be resolved in the foreseeable future. What is clear, however, is that modernization introduced technologies such as dynamite, modern transportation systems, and new and more lethal weapons, all of which terrorists have exploited to their advantage.

THE IMPACT OF GLOBALIZATION

Globalization is one of the most important concepts of modern times. It can be defined as the global integration of markets, nation states, technologies, and goods to an unprecedented level. Globalization is characterized by the spread of free enterprise, exchange of information, information technology, and free movement of capital and people that affects nearly every corner of the globe. Globalization also affects nearly every aspect of human life, including politics, economics, warfare, and culture. As Thomas Friedman of the *New York Times* put it, globalization enables individuals, corporations, and states to "reach around the world farther, faster, deeper, and cheaper," and enables the world to reach into "individuals, corporations, and nation-states farther, faster, deeper, and cheaper." [91] Globalization has been recognized as one of the central forces of our time and the foreseeable future. A recent report by the National Intelligence Council described globalization as an overarching "mega-trend," a force so ubiquitous that it will substantially shape all the other major trends in the world through the year 2020. [92]

As with modernization, the effects of globalization on societies are not clear-cut. Supporters of globalization argue that its benefits outnumber its risks. Globalization, they maintain, brings different societies and economies closer to one another, and will eventually make poorer countries wealthier. These advocates of globalization see trade as a catalyst of development and regard globalization as a means to fighting poverty.

Critics argue that globalization excludes the vast majority of people and creates a separate global class that speaks English and has access to the modern technologies—such as Internet access, fax, e-mail, and satellite television—which enables the members of this elite to communicate among themselves. As a result, income disparities lead to the decline of the working classes and the poor. Those who are unable to benefit from globalization are alienated and disoriented, because globalization disintegrates their traditional cultural communities.[93]

As to globalization's effect on terrorism, researchers using statistical data on 112 countries demonstrated that trade and foreign investments—the economic hallmarks of globalization—have "no direct positive effect on transnational terrorist incidents within countries." Instead, they found that the economic development of a country reduces the number of terrorist incidents inside the country.[94] Like poverty, then, globalization does not seem to have a direct effect in creating more terrorism.

However, there are indications that globalization has an indirect effect on terrorism. First, globalization may produce the social and psychological conditions that can lead to terrorism. Globalization may be weakening the traditional nation-state by shifting people's identities from national to ethnic and religious orientations. An individual from the Iraqi city of Mosul, for example, may see himself as a Kurd or a Muslim first and as an Iraqi citizen second. Likewise, a person from the northern part of Sri Lanka may regard herself as Buddhist or an ethnic Tamil before she considers herself a Sri Lankan. This shift of identities is fertile soil for violent xenophobia toward those who are believed to be a danger to the traditional cultures.[95]

Second, disparities produced by globalization help terrorist groups recruit new members. Globalization has raised the

In this photograph, anti-globalization demonstrators march in New York City in March 2002. These demonstrators protested retailers engaged in global sweatshop manufacturing, one of the major complaints of globalization's critics.

absolute standard of living across the globe. It has also, however, increased the gap between rich and poor in the process.[96] This has enabled groups like al Qaeda to justify their terrorism as a legitimate struggle against Western oppression. Such groups are not necessarily concerned with the economic plight of those whom they mobilize, but it is easier for them to recruit a person who has resentments than a person who is content in life.

Third, whether justified or not, the United States is identified by many people in the poorer regions of the world as the source of globalization. Critics of globalization maintain that Western economic investments in poor countries often lead to political and economic turmoil. They sometimes charge multi-national corporations (MNCs) such as Nike with exploiting cheap local labor in so-called sweatshops. The critics also accuse MNCs of withdrawing from countries at will, leaving them to their own devices. Abandoning countries after helping them, those critics say, may breed terrorists.

Others perceive globalization as a form of cultural imperialism, whereby the United States is trying to impose its popular culture of McDonald's, MTV, and Starbucks upon societies that wish to preserve their traditional cultures. The cultural imposition is widely perceived as a forced introduction of Western values such as consumerism, individualism, competition, and mobility. These alien, liberal concepts clash with the values prevalent in many traditional societies, such as obligation to the community, family, respect, shared resources, and patriarchal family and social structures. Communities may also feel that their local language is endangered by the spread of English. Of course, these processes do not necessarily lead to terrorism. In their totality, however, they produce an atmosphere of social and cultural dislocation among communities that a movement such as al Qaeda can cynically exploit—a movement whose upper echelons ironically often share many of the traits of the "globalized" individual, including a high level of education, multilingualism, and computer expertise.

Fourth, the technological and social changes introduced by the West through globalization are being used against it. Globalization requires high productivity and efficiency. Travelers, for instance, can quickly board airplanes using e-tickets rather than paper tickets. Over time, many countries have also relaxed their limitations on immigration to support their economies. Though these changes have helped transform the world into a "global village," they have also enabled terrorists to move around more easily.

Terrorists have often used inventions originally designed for peaceful purposes to help them carry out acts of violence. Alfred Nobel's invention of dynamite in 1866, for example, was supposed to revolutionize the construction business, not terrorism. In the end, it did both. Many anarchist groups, including some in the United States, began using dynamite to terrorize their political opponents. Likewise, the terrorist activities of the anarchist organization Narodnaya Volya (the People's Will), exploited Russia's newly established railway system for its own ends. Similarly, a Palestinian terrorist group, the PFLP, saw the rise in air travel as an opportunity to introduce an innovative new terrorist tactic in 1968—civilian airline hijacking. Terrorists also exploit the Internet to spread their hateful messages, raise funds, and even recruit new members.

A fifth way in which globalization has an indirect effect on terrorism relates to the organizational structure of terrorist groups. Some of the changes introduced by globalization have enabled the formation of a new generation of terrorist organization—terrorist networks—which pose a serious threat to Western countries and their allies around the globe. Unlike traditional terrorist groups, terrorist networks are not hierarchically structured, nor are they concentrated in a certain region. Instead, they are geographically dispersed, which is why the new terror networks, of which al Qaeda is the prime example, are also known as transnational networks. Transnational terror networks are extremely shadowy, little is known about their precise leadership structure, and they have no headquarters.[97] The network is organized in cells, each consisting of as few as 2 and as many as 15 members. Al Qaeda, for example, is believed to have cells in approximately 100 countries.[98]

How is the structure of the transnational terrorist networks an outgrowth of globalization? These networks are dependent on the modern technologies characteristic of globalization: cellular and satellite phones, fax machines, laptop computers, news networks such as CNN, and e-mail. Transnational networks would not exist if it were not for the ease of travel in modern times. Networks also use modern means of communication to exchange messages across continents quickly and inexpensively. Al Qaeda, for example, uses steganography—the process of putting encrypted messages in electronic files—to pass messages, including instructions for attacks, from one cell to another.[99]

Globalization is a complex phenomenon that offers both opportunities and risks. While globalization, or modernization, cannot by itself be blamed for the occurrence of terrorism, it does render societies more vulnerable by enabling terrorist organizations to be more effective. Hendrik Hertzberg described the relationship between globalization and terrorism well when he wrote that "in the decade since the end of the Cold War, the human race has become, with increasing rapidity, a single organism. Every kind of barrier to the free and rapid movement of goods, information, and people has been lowered. The organism relies increasingly on a kind of trust. . . . The terrorists made use of that trust. They rode the flow of the world's aerial circulatory system like lethal viruses."[100]

SUMMARY

Economics, modernization, and globalization are crucial for a proper understanding of terrorism and its causes. While poverty does not lead directly to terrorism, there are indirect links between poverty and terrorism. Poor countries often provide safe havens for terrorism; poverty can lead to civil war, which in turn breeds terrorism; and poverty makes it easier for terrorist groups to recruit members.

It has been shown that terrorism can at times become a business, enriching terrorist leaders while providing ordinary terrorist members with an additional incentive—indeed, sometimes the primary motivation—to remain in the group; namely, earning money.

There is no consensus on whether or not modernization is causing terrorism. Some have argued that rapid modernization is detrimental to a country's stability, polarizing the population by making the rich richer and leaving the poor with less. At the same time, we cannot escape the fact that terrorism has occurred in many "modern" countries, including the United States and most of Western Europe. Hence, modernization as an explanation of terrorism is not satisfying.

Finally, we looked at whether globalization has a positive or negative effect on terrorism. As with poverty, globalization is not directly responsible for "causing terrorism." In fact, globalization carries with it many opportunities. But globalization may indirectly strengthen terrorists in several ways: by confusing the identities of individuals, making them more susceptible to recruitment by terrorist organizations; by expanding the divide between rich and poor, making it easier for terrorist groups to recruit the disenchanted masses; by its association with cultural imperialism, which is perceived to threaten the traditional local culture; by creating technologies that terrorist groups can use against the West; and by enabling terrorist organizations to morph from hierarchical organizations into more threatening terrorist networks.

Trade, investment, modernization, and globalization create opportunities and vulnerabilities. The challenge for Western countries like the United States will be to strike the right balance between the opportunities globalization is believed to entail—free markets, an unlimited flow of information, education, and a rise in living standards—while safeguarding and respecting the indigenous cultures that all too often feel threatened by the powerful forces of a seemingly unstoppable global interconnectedness.

CHAPTER 6

SOCIETY, CULTURE, AND TERRORISM

On September 11, 2001, the United States suffered the most deadly terrorist attack ever committed on its soil, and the most devastating surprise attack against American targets since the Japanese assault on Pearl Harbor. At first, many thought that the suicide hijackers must have been young, neglected, and poor individuals who acted out of desperation, as if they had nothing to lose. Americans and non-Americans alike, however, were soon surprised to learn that while the attackers were indeed young, they were far from socially disadvantaged and even farther from being poor. Muhammad Atta, the suicide pilot of the first aircraft that hit the World Trade Center, was a 33-year-old student at the Technical University in Hamburg, Germany. Atta was a seemingly intelligent and educated man whom a former professor described as "pious . . . yet not fanatical," a "critical spirit . . . who even argued in favor of religious coexistence."[101] Some of Atta's fellow suicide hijackers came from Saudi Arabia and the United Arab Emirates, two of the most affluent Arab countries. Indeed, the hijackers were not raised in an atmosphere of perpetual conflict or poverty.

This chapter examines the social, cultural, and historical context of terrorism by addressing several questions: Is there a sociological profile of the individual terrorist? What are some of the common societal explanations for the causes of terrorism? Is terrorism rooted in a society's culture? Do historical narratives common to a society have any effect on terrorism?

IS THERE A TYPICAL TERRORIST PROFILE?

Several studies have shown that, on average, the active member of a terrorist group is 20–25 years old. In many countries, though, terrorist groups are recruiting adolescents, and even children.[102] At times, terrorist groups force children to join rebellions and terrorist attacks. The Liberation Tigers of Tamil Eelam (LTTE), a group fighting for a separate state of ethnic Tamils in Sri Lanka, has taken children as young as 12 out of their homes and forced them to join the Tiger's ranks.[103]

Terrorist leaders, by contrast, tend to be older. Osama bin Laden was in his mid 40s when his al Qaeda operatives took control of the four U.S. airliners on 9/11. Carlos Marighella, the main theorist of the urban guerrilla strategy, was 58 when he was killed in 1969. Shoko Asahara, the leader of the Japanese Aum Shinrikyo cult, was 40 when his disciples released sarin nerve gas in the Tokyo subway system.

The radical left-wing organizations of Western Europe such as the Red Army Faction or the Red Brigades, as well as the Japanese Red Army, were characterized by a relatively small membership that came mostly from the middle-class and sometimes the upper-middle class. Members of organizations with a relatively large membership, such as the Provisional

IRA, the Revolutionary Armed Forces of Columbia (FARC), the Kurdistan Workers Party (PKK), and the LTTE, as well as radical Islamist groups in the West Bank and Gaza, are mostly drawn from the working class or from among the very poor. Leaders of these organizations, in contrast, tend to come from the middle and upper classes.[104]

Terrorists also tend to be single, though there are exceptions. On September 9, 2001, for example, 48-year-old Muhammad Shaker Habeishi detonated a bomb at a train station in the northern Israeli town of Nahariya, killing himself and three other Israelis. Habeishi was married and the father of eight children.[105] Carlos the Jackal, perhaps the most well-known terrorist of the 1970s and 1980s, described himself in 1994 as a revolutionary and "above all a family man."[106]

Finally, most terrorists are male. A recent study on the terrorist organization Basque Homeland and Freedom (ETA), a group that fights for an independent Basque homeland in Spain, confirmed that about 90% of ETA members are men. "Contemporary terrorism is predominantly a male phenomenon," concluded the author of that study, providing two explanations. First, men are prone to aggressive behavior in general and terrorism in particular; and second, male-dominated and patriarchal cultures often influence terrorism.[107]

Most terrorism experts have concluded that although some general tendencies can be identified, there is no single terrorist profile. Apart from the general tendency of terrorists to be male and young, no personality traits have yet been identified that might help law enforcement authorities detect terrorists in advance. Terrorists behave, dress, and look like ordinary persons, a fact that makes terrorist profiling based on personality traits or physical appearance useless.

SOCIETAL EXPLANATIONS OF VIOLENCE

Sociological explanations of terrorism are those that take into account the role that the social environment has on the behavior

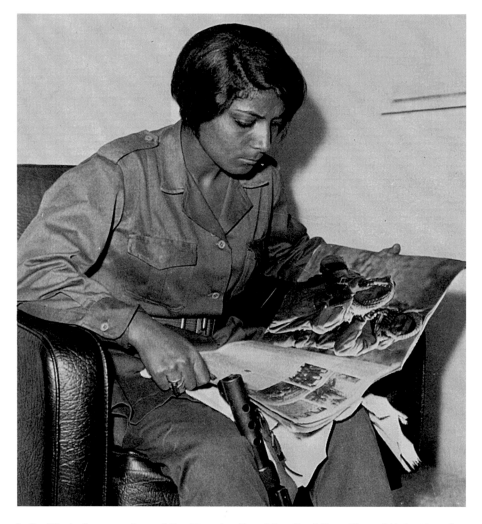

Leila Khaled, a member of the Popular Front for the Liberation of Palestine, is pictured here at the age of 24. Khaled helped hijack a TWA passenger plane on August 29, 1969, inspiring future female terrorists.

of the individual. A social environment could, for example, be characterized by social, political, and economic inequalities between groups of people, and in turn affect the individual's willingness to engage in terrorism.

Of the various sociological theories to explain the roots of violence, including terrorism, two theories are particularly well

Female Terrorists

Women have played an active role in the modern history of political terrorism, and at times have even assumed a leadership role. One of the first female terrorists was Leila Khaled, a member of the Popular Front for the Liberation of Palestine (PFLP), who helped hijack a TWA passenger plane on August 29, 1969. Her persona inspired generations of subsequent female terrorists.

Roughly a third of the members of Germany's Red Army Faction—and an even higher percentage of the group's supporters—were women. In Italy, women accounted for about 20 percent of those arrested for terrorism between 1970 and 1984. Women also played a key role in Latin American insurgent groups such as Peru's Sendero Luminoso (Shining Path) or Nicaragua's Sandinista National Liberation Front (FSLN).

Most recently, Sri Lankan, Palestinian, and Chechen women terrorists have gained notoriety for their willingness to die as suicide bombers. In recent years, the use of women terrorists, including suicide bombers, has increased sharply. A major reason for this rise is practical: Women generally arouse less suspicion than men. Various female terrorists, for example, have posed as "pregnant" women in order to avoid intrusive security measures. Organizations are also known to take advantage of the desire of many women who want to prove their commitment to the group and their cause.

Some researchers have suggested that a distinctive psychology applies to women terrorists, including their experience of a weak mother, a tyrannical father, a higher idealism, feminism, and the search for companionship in a group. Others have argued that women have a "maternal-sacrificial code"—a natural tendency to protect and sacrifice themselves for their children. In the case of female terrorists, this code translates into a willingness to sacrifice themselves for the organization. Most researchers, however, do not believe that there are substantive distinctions between motivations for women to become terrorists compared to the motivations for men.

known. The first is Johan Galtung's "structural violence,"[108] which states that political and economic inequalities between different groups within a society cause harm to the disadvantaged group. Structural violence is different from physical or direct violence, which cause harm with fists or weapons. Structural violence causes suffering in the form of poverty, hunger, homelessness, oppression, or discrimination. It can occur whenever a group of people—often women, children, the elderly, or groups from different ethnic, racial, and religious backgrounds and sexual orientations—lack equal access to political, legal, economic, educational, health, and other resources to which the mainstream has access. Structural violence does not necessarily lead to physical violence, but in extreme cases it can create unrest, terrorism, or even genocide. In Northern Ireland, for example, marked economic and educational discrepancies between Catholics and Protestants contributed to the emergence of terrorism. In Rwanda, striking inequalities between the two major ethnic communities, the Hutus and the Tutsis, contributed to the genocide that ravaged the country between April and December 1994, killing half a million to a million people.[109]

A variation of structural violence is the relative deprivation (RD) theory developed by Ted Robert Gurr.[110] According to this theory, wide gaps between people's political, economic, and personal expectations and the satisfaction of these goals form the basic condition that leads to collective violence. The larger the gap between what people want to achieve—personal richness, power, status, or health—and what they are able to achieve given their circumstances, the higher the likelihood that they will engage in violent activities. RD leads first to frustration of the group and subsequently to aggression. Although RD has been criticized by some terrorism analysts, others believe that the concept helps explain terrorism in certain cases. One expert on suicide terrorism, for example, argues that "support and recruitment for suicide terrorism occur . . . when converging political, economic, and social trends produce diminishing opportunities relative to expectations, thus generating frustrations that radical organizations can exploit."[111]

CULTURAL ASPECTS OF TERRORISM

The question of whether or not terrorism is a cultural phenomenon has long been debated. Traditions such as revenge, blood feuds, and clan-based warfare are common to certain regions of the world such as the Caucasus, Central Asia, the Middle East, and North Africa. These traditions may in part explain violence in some of these regions.[112]

Before we consider this view, however, we must first define culture. Culture refers to meanings, values, and behavioral norms that have been transmitted to a certain group of people over time. Culture affects the way people behave, communicate with one another, and look at various aspects of life. Culture is a learned phenomenon and hence not part of the human genetic code. Many Americans, for instance, like to eat cereal and milk in the morning. The desire for milk and cereal is not a genetic response or an instinct, but rather a learned response. Another such learned response is the native language that we speak—our mother tongue—which also constitutes part of our culture.

There are several ways culture can help us understand terrorism and its causes.[113] First, it can help us understand more about the motivations of terrorists by placing the terrorist and the act of terrorism in a specific cultural context. One example are the Chechnya-based terrorist groups that have staged numerous attacks, including suicide bombings, against Russian civilian and military personnel. The Chechens are a predominantly Muslim ethnic group that has lived for centuries in the mountainous Caucasus region. While there are many reasons why Chechen terrorist groups have adopted terrorist violence, a major one is the immense loss of Chechen lives that resulted from Russian attacks. Tens of thousands of Chechens have been killed in two violent wars between Chechnya and Russia, in the wake of which Grozny, the Chechen capital, has been completely destroyed. Chechens have responded with guerrilla and terrorist attacks that in turn killed at least 5,000, but probably a higher number, of Russian soldiers, as well as hundreds of civilians.[114] Personal grievances such as the loss of family members, friends, or a home—hundreds of thousands of Chechens have been displaced—play a large role in encouraging Chechen terrorism. In addition to such grievances, Chechens also have a culture of resistance. Throughout their history, the Chechens have resisted Russian attempts to subjugate their homeland. So, Chechen cultural tradition, ingrained with resistance, is likely to play a role as an additional motivating element in the use of terrorist tactics.

Second, culture can help us understand the behavior and core beliefs of a terrorist group. Considering the historical and symbolic references that a particular terrorist organization uses in its statements, terrorism analysts can gain better insight into the workings of the group, which may improve the ability of governments to reduce the threat posed by specific terrorist organizations. Of key importance here is understanding how these groups view themselves in terms of ethnicity, religion, or nationality, and their relationship with the host culture. In the case of the al Qaeda movement, for example, its adherents subscribe to a radical version of the ideology of Islamism. Radical Islamists believe that all Muslims are under attack by the West, led by the United States, which has embarked on a crusade against Muslims (see Chapter 7). Al Qaeda also believes that in order to resist this Western attack, Muslims must participate in a holy struggle to defeat the "infidels," a struggle that must be fought at all times. Knowledge of al Qaeda's core beliefs and behavior—its culture—helps governments understand that al Qaeda entertains absolute goals, is unwilling to compromise, and regards its struggle against all "infidels," especially the West, as protracted.

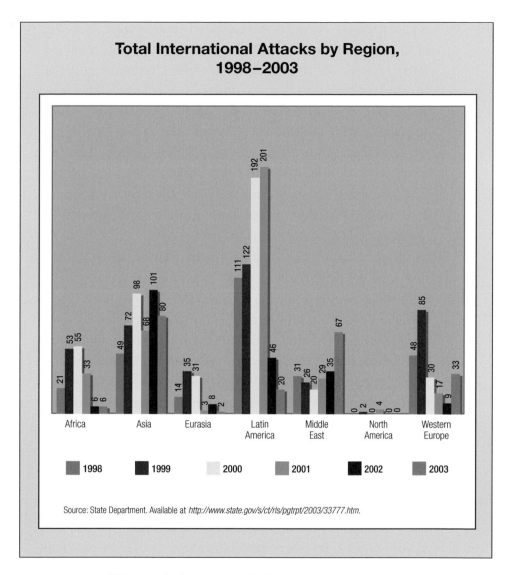

Table 6.1 This graph, from the U.S. State Department's Website, shows the number of international terrorist attacks in different regions of the world from 1998 to 2003.

Third, culture can help us understand the broader meaning behind a particular act of terrorism. What does the act of terrorism symbolize to the perpetrator, the organization, and the society in which the organization operates? On 9/11, al Qaeda chose to strike at the leading military and financial nerve centers of the United States—the Pentagon and the World Trade Center—among other targets. To the followers of al Qaeda, these landmarks represented the planning headquarters of what they see as the American offensive against the Muslim world. By striking the targets that best embody the power of the United States, the act of terrorism symbolizes to al Qaeda and its sympathizers not an evil deed but rather a long-awaited blow at the superpower that, in the eyes of al Qaeda, is trying to enslave the Muslim world.

Fourth, culture may help shed light on how certain groups and societies justify acts of terrorism. The widespread public support among Palestinians for suicide bombings in the West Bank and Gaza is a case in point. "Martyrdom operations," as suicide attacks are commonly called among Palestinians, have long since reached the status of a pop culture in Gaza and the West Bank. In September 2001, for instance, An-Najah University in the West Bank town of Nablus sponsored an exhibition on martyrdom operations that featured reenactments of suicide bombings. In the streets of Gaza, young children reenact suicide bombings in a game called *shuhada* (martyrdom), which even includes a mock funeral, while teenaged rock groups sing songs praising the latest martyrdom operation. Asked to name their heroes, young Palestinians often mention suicide bombers—known as *shaheeds* (martyrs)—rather than music or television stars. This "cult" of the suicide bomber is among the most important reasons why there seems to be a steady flow of Palestinians willing to sacrifice themselves.[115] For many affected by the culture of death prevalent in Gaza and the West Bank, becoming a suicide bomber is a great honor and *shaheeds* typically become celebrities after their deaths. "The overwhelming cultural message," Giovanni Caracci, a professor of psychiatry at the New Jersey Medical School, notes, "is that immolating oneself to destroy other lives is not only acceptable but highly

In this 1993 photograph, Palestinian children are shown throwing rocks at an Israeli army base. Many Palestinians support action against Israeli presence in disputed territories, and often pass these sentiments on to their children.

desirable. . . . They will be heroes in everyone's eyes, will have helped the [Palestinian] cause, and will be rewarded in the afterlife. There is no known antidote to this culturally sanctioned meaning of such extreme forms of violence . . . unless it comes from within the culture itself."[116]

Fifth, cultural aspects may influence the response by the larger society to an act of terrorism perpetrated by a group within that society. This is especially true for nationalistically or religiously motivated terrorist groups, which depend heavily on their larger society's moral and practical support. The Provisional IRA, for example, is believed to have several thousand local and international sympathizers. In the case of al Qaeda, social support in the Arab and Muslim world for this radical Islamist movement is widespread. A 2003 poll conducted by the Pew Research Center found that in several Arab and Muslim countries, including Jordan, Indonesia, Morocco, Pakistan, and the Palestinian Authority, between 44 percent and 71 percent of respondents had a favorable view of Osama bin Laden.[117] Anti-American resentment runs deep in many Arab and Muslim countries, where America is widely perceived to be anti-Muslim, culturally corrupt, and pro-Israel in its policy. Meanwhile, religious schools in Pakistan and Afghanistan, known as *madrassahs*, preach hatred of the West and indoctrinate their students with radical versions of Islam.

NARRATIVES AND THE HISTORICAL CONTEXT OF TERRORISM

Understanding cultural aspects of a particular society can help us understand why some communities, when under pressure, produce violent acts, while others may not. The remainder of this chapter will address whether and how historical memories— of injustices by a tyrannical ruler, for example, or the effects of foreign occupation—as well as legends, myths, and other narratives, influence the emergence of terrorism, its persistence, and its nature. To gain a better understanding of the roots of terrorism, an awareness of the historical context of a particular community or society is important because groups are often motivated not only by the present, but also by what has happened in the past. Ethnic communities and entire nations may have been subjected to genocide or dispossessed of their homelands. Those past traumatic events often have a significant effect on the culture of that particular society and, ultimately, on its manifestations of terrorism.

Narratives are particularly important because the telling of stories is the main way in which historical events are transmitted through generations. Narratives contain powerful images that help turn historical events into symbols, and thus help place a special meaning on a particular event. For Americans, for instance, July 4, 1776, symbolizes more than the date on which the United States declared its independence. It was a historic milestone that symbolized the victory of values such as life, liberty, and the pursuit of happiness. To most Americans, 1776 has remained a powerful symbol because generations of Americans have transmitted the significance of this event to subsequent generations through personal stories, songs, rituals, or books.

Narratives reveal to us how certain groups and communities look at the world that surrounds them. Narratives can also help us understand the deep fears and perceived threats, as well as social and political grievances, that are common within a society. Finally, narratives can provide a window into understanding how these societies believe they should react to a certain threat—be it through passive resistance, non-violence, or terrorism.[118]

Khalchig Tololyan demonstrated the importance of literature, religion, and narratives using the example of an Armenian terrorist group, the Armenian Secret Army for the Liberation of Armenia (ASALA). Tololyan argued that Armenians in general have a tradition of resistance rooted in 15 centuries of popular discourse and narrative, church rituals, and even songs. That tradition is passed on in churches, schools, athletic unions, and student groups,which sustain a certain culture in a community that has been without an independent sovereign homeland for much of its history. A major part of the Armenian narrative is the story of the massacre of Armenians by the so-called Young Turks during 1915–1916.[119]

The pain of victimhood felt by groups that have suffered injustices can strongly affect the likelihood of conflict, including terrorism. Victimization often results from personal experience and represents part of a historic and ongoing threat that is perceived to emanate from an adversary group. The slaughter of the Armenians at the height of World War I, therefore, is an example of how past victimhood can continue to affect an ongoing sense of threat. Ever since the mass killings were committed, the Armenian community has insisted that the massacres constituted a genocide, the deliberate killing of people based on their ethnicity, nationality, race, or religion.[120] Turkey refuses to label the killings using this term and claims that the number of victims is far smaller than the 1.5 million figure that most Armenians cite. Many Armenians believe that Turkey's failure to acknowledge the extent of the killings—by refusing to label it "genocide"—means that future killings of Armenians are possible.[121]

Another contemporary example in which the historical context and stories play an important role is the Israeli–Palestinian conflict. Both Israelis and Palestinians are influenced by narratives that portray their own group as righteous and the other group as the sole culprit. Both sides are also affected by their more recent tormented past. From the Palestinian perspective, that recent past includes the loss of their homeland to an alien people in 1948, when the state of Israel was created—an event that Palestinians refer to as *Nakba* (catastrophe). Palestinians also share a collective memory of several decades of an Israeli occupation that left them frustrated and humiliated. Curfews, military roadblocks, detentions, and a general lack of opportunities have left entire generations of Palestinians all but hopeless. In 1987, Palestinians in the occupied territories began a violent resistance (*intifada*) to the Israeli occupation, thus exacerbating the enmity between Palestinians and Israelis.

Meanwhile, Israeli historical narratives focus on the persecution of Jews throughout history and on their ability to survive against the odds. Jews in general lament the loss of their first and second temple, their subsequent expulsion from the land that is now Israel, and centuries of anti-Semitism that culminated in the Nazi Holocaust, the systematic murder of 6 million Jews. For most Jews and Israelis, the lesson of the Holocaust is "never again"—a slogan that explains the need for Jewish self-defense and invokes historical examples of Jewish resistance and revolt.

SUMMARY

Cultural traditions shaped by centuries of struggle and transmitted with the help of narratives that place resistance, struggle, and martyrdom in a heroic light are "able to produce and sustain a certain level of terrorist activity."[122] The historical context is an important element in the formation of such cultural foundations. It is for that reason that we have to take a society's historical experience with oppression and resistance into account, as it helps us understand the formation of groups willing to use violence as a tool to achieve their goals.

There are numerous societies where violence and resistance have been part of their collective history. Such cultures influenced by narratives of both suffering and resistance are not limited to Armenians, Palestinians, or Jews. In fact, cultural traditions where violence, resistance to oppression, and heroic death in battle are prominent features of communal consciousness, transmitted through the generations using stories and legends, are found virtually everywhere.

CHAPTER 7

RELIGIOUS EXPLANATIONS OF TERRORISM

On March 20, 1995, five men equipped with umbrellas and loosely wrapped newspapers boarded several trains at opposite ends of the Tokyo subway system. When the trains converged at the Kasumigaseki Station in the center of the Japanese capital, the men took out plastic sacks from the newspapers, punctured them with the sharpened tips of their umbrellas, and exited the cars. After a few minutes, the passengers in the wagons began vomiting, convulsing, and collapsing. They had suffered the horrible effects of exposure to sarin, the nerve gas that the five men had released.

About a month later in the United States, on April 19, 1995, a Ryder rental truck exploded in front of the Alfred P. Murrah Federal Building in Oklahoma City. The enormous blast destroyed the entire front of the building, which served as the regional headquarters for various agencies affiliated with the federal government. In the explosion, 168 people were killed and over 500 were injured, among them many children. At that time, the Oklahoma City bombing, as the attack came to be known, was the most fatal terrorist attack to take place on U.S. soil. Its destructiveness and cost in human lives has been overshadowed only by the events of September 11, 2001.

What the Tokyo subway, Oklahoma City, and September 11 attacks have in common is that the groups responsible for each were motivated in large part by religion. Religiously motivated terrorism is now the most widespread and lethal form of terrorism.[123] This, however, has not always been the case. In 1980, for example, the United States identified only one terrorist organization that was religious in character. By 1998, half of the groups that the U.S. Secretary of State listed as "most dangerous" were religious. Today, the number of terrorist groups espousing religious goals is even higher.[124]

We should keep in mind that religious terrorism should not be viewed as completely separate from other forms of terrorism. Religious terrorism, for example, is usually also politically motivated. Following the U.S.-led invasion of Iraq in 2003, for instance, radical Islamist organizations (as well as other groups) embarked on a sustained campaign of guerrilla and terrorist attacks against the United States and its allies. Its demands, however, were not only religious, but also political—they wanted the United States to withdraw its troops from Iraq. Therefore, when we think about religious terrorism, we should think of terrorism that is largely, though not only, motivated by religion.

RELIGIOUS TERRORISM IN HISTORY

Nearly all religions of the world have produced religious terrorists, including Christianity, Islam, Judaism, Hinduism, and Buddhism. Religiously based terrorism is as old as history itself, and prior to the nineteenth century, religion was the main justification used for terrorism.[125]

One of the earliest groups to stage religiously motivated attacks was a radical Jewish sect known as the *Sicarii*, or dagger-men. Using a primitive version of a dagger (*sica*), members of this group killed Roman legionnaires who occupied the region then known as Judea. The Sicarii also killed Jewish citizens whom they accused of siding with the Romans, thus betraying their Jewish brethren and their faith.

Religious terrorism was also common in India. The word "thug" is derived from a group that committed acts of religious terror in India beginning in the seventh century. Using nooses, the *thuggee* killed innocent victims, believing that these acts would serve Kali, the Hindu goddess of terror and destruction. Until they were suppressed in the mid-nineteenth century, the thugs killed an estimated one million people, more than any other terrorist group in history.

Terror was also a widespread tactic used by the medieval Christian Crusaders. In 1097, Crusaders catapulted the severed heads of Turkish corpses into the town of Nicaea, in Asia Minor. When the first Crusade reached Jerusalem in 1099, the Crusaders staged a five-week-long siege that was followed by a massacre of Jerusalem's Jewish and Muslim populations. The Crusaders' goal was to turn Jerusalem into a purely Christian city.

After the French Revolution in 1789, terrorism motivated by religion became a less common phenomenon. The late eighteenth and early nineteenth centuries gave rise to more secular ideologies, such as nationalism and Marxism. These ideologies also affected terrorism, which was increasingly justified in secular terms. From around 1800 to the late 1970s, most terrorist attacks were perpetrated either by nationalist groups or by groups that espoused radical political, not religious, ideologies.

Religious terrorism gained new impetus with the Islamic Revolution that swept Iran in 1979. Indeed, the effects of this event are still felt in the Middle East and elsewhere today.

When modern religious terrorism reared its head after the 1979 revolution, most attacks initially were perpetrated by radical Islamist groups such as Hizbollah, a radical organization in Lebanon based on Shiism, a form of Islam that is most dominant in Iran and Iraq. However, a few years after the Iranian revolution, religious terrorism was adopted by groups from other religions as well as more obscure sects and cults. Today,

The Assassins

The word *assassination* today describes a sudden and treacherous attack, usually involving the murder of an individual, such as that of President John F. Kennedy in 1963. A lesser known fact is that the word comes from the name of a medieval Muslim group, the "Assassins," a radical sect that spread fear and horror around parts of the Middle East between the eleventh and thirteenth centuries.

The Assassins were an obscure group belonging to the Ismaili branch of Shia Islam. In the late eleventh century, Hassan-i Sabbah, the leader of the Ismailis, seized the castle of Alamut in the Alburz mountains south of the Caspian Sea and established a group of devoted followers to help him spread the Ismaili version of Shiism across the Middle East. They became known as the Assassins.

The Assassins regarded themselves as messengers of God. Their preferred tactic was to kill the leaders of their enemies, which included all those who resisted the Assassins' attempts to convert the "non-believers." The Assassins' weapon of choice was the dagger, which they used to kill their enemies in broad daylight, even in the presence of their bodyguards. The Assassins rarely attempted to escape from the scene after stabbing their victims to death. This seemingly fanatical courage of the Assassins gave birth to the myth that the Assassins were drugged with hashish, a belief that gave the Assassins (*Hashashiyoun* or *Hashishiyyin* in Arabic) their name. Today, however, most modern scholars of the Assassins believe the story about the use of hashish to be untrue. The Assassins were eventually wiped out during the Mongol invasion of the Middle East in the thirteenth century.

few, if any, religions are immune from at least some terrorist elements in their midst.

THE NATURE OF RELIGIOUS TERRORISM

Religious terrorism differs in several important respects from other types of terrorism. First, religious terrorism has resulted, on average, in much higher fatalities than terrorism committed primarily for nationalist or ideological reasons. As we have seen, nearly 3,000 people were killed in the attacks of 9/11. Thousands of other casualties have resulted from religiously motivated terrorist attacks in places as diverse as Spain, Russia, Israel, Morocco, Turkey, Indonesia, Yemen, Saudi Arabia, and Pakistan.

Second, religious terrorists define their targets in relatively broad terms and tend to strike at highly symbolic targets. Members of other religions—or even of other sects within the same religion—are regarded by religious terrorists as "non-believers" and hence as legitimate targets. Religious terrorists select symbolic targets carefully in order to maximize the psychological trauma of the target population and to appear powerful in the eyes of their constituency and their enemies. A prime example of such symbolic targeting are the attacks of 9/11, in which al Qaeda hit the military and economic nerve centers of the United States. Politically motivated groups, in contrast, tend to concentrate their attacks on more specific targets such as political, business, or military leaders. Killing as many people as possible is not necessarily in the interest of politically motivated terrorists, whose main goal often is to instill fear and draw attention to their cause.

Third, religious terrorists consider the use of violence to be a holy act perpetrated in accordance with divine will. Such a rationalization of violence may be the result of religious belief. At the same time, by invoking a higher source of authority, terrorists are able to obtain the "moral permission" to engage in violence. Religious terrorists often assert that they are merely defending themselves against aggression. They frequently

Above, American soldiers march in formation in Saudi Arabia. The presence of American troops near the Muslim holy cities of Mecca and Medina (both in Saudi Arabia) has long been a source of tension between Muslims and the United States.

perceive their religious community to be under attack, either militarily, politically, or culturally. Al Qaeda, for instance, has cited U.S. military presence in Saudi Arabia—the location of Islam's holy cities Mecca and Medina—as a threat to Islam, and has used this to justify their attacks against the United States.

Fourth, religious terrorists generally frame their struggle against their victims in absolute terms. Religious terrorists believe that God is on their side and that they are engaged in a total war of good against evil. Frequently, such black-and-white views are enforced by the way that the group perceives its community's past. Religious terrorists tend to invoke only the favorable images of their historic past, such as glorious triumphs in major military battles or the past possession of large swaths of territory. When compared to the usually more somber and less glorious reality in which the religious terrorists find themselves at present, a selective view of their past can encourage them to attempt to reinstate past glories by using violence.[126]

Fifth, religious terrorists seem less concerned about influencing an outside audience than do politically motivated terrorists. Political terrorist organizations such as the IRA, for example, generally refrain from employing large-scale violence because public opinion is very important to them. For religious terrorists, convincing an audience that their cause is just is not a high priority goal. It is the act of violence itself—perpetrated "in defense" of their religion—that is the goal in itself.

Finally, religious terrorists differ from secular terrorists in the scale of their goals. The goals of secular groups such as the IRA are limited. Were the IRA, for instance, to succeed in their goals of removing British forces from Northern Ireland and unifying Ireland, then presumably the IRA would no longer have any reason to continue using violence. For religious terrorists, however, the struggle against the "infidels" is almost limitless, and fulfilling the absolute demands of religious terrorist groups is very difficult.[127] Battles waged by religious terrorists are likely to be enduring.

THE ROOTS OF RELIGIOUS TERRORISM

Experts on terrorism and religion have put forward a number of explanations for the rise in religious violence, including terrorism. First, it is important to examine the connection between violence and religion.

Although religion is often associated with positive values such as compassion and peace, the mythology of most world

MAJOR ATTACKS ATTRIBUTED TO AL QAEDA AND ITS AFFILIATES

Date	Attack	Fatalities
25 June 1996	Truck bombing at the U.S. military's housing facility at Khobar Towers; Dhahran, Saudi Arabia	19
7 August 1998	Car bombing at the U.S. embassies in Kenya and Tanzania	303
12 October 2000	Suicide boat bombing against the American destroyer USS *Cole*; Aden, Yemen	17
11 September 2001	Suicide hijacking of four American airliners, including two flown into New York's World Trade Center and one into the Pentagon in Washington, D.C.	2,986
11 April 2002	Truck bomb at synagogue in Djerba, Tunisia	21
8 May 2002	Car bomb driven into a minibus carrying French naval technicians; Karachi, Pakistan	13
17 June 2002	Car bomb exploding outside the U.S. consulate in Karachi, Pakistan	11
12 October 2002	The al Qaeda-affiliated Jemaah Islamiyyah detonates a suicide car bomb at a nightclub in Bali, Indonesia	202
28 November 2002	Suicide car bomb against the Israeli-owned Paradise Hotel; Mombasa, Kenya	15
12 May 2003	Suicide car bombs hit three expatriate compounds in Riyadh, Saudi Arabia	34
16 May 2003	Multiple suicide bombings in Casablanca, Morocco, including a Spanish restaurant, a Jewish-owned Italian restaurant, a Jewish cemetary, a Kuwaiti-owned hotel, and a Jewish community center	16
20 August 2003	Al Qaeda-related Ansar al-Islam drives suicide truck bomb into the UN headquarters in Baghdad, Iraq	19
15 November 2003	Two Jewish synagogues are attacked with suicide car bombs in Istanbul, Turkey	23
20 November 2003	UK Consulate and HSBC Bank building in Istanbul are attacked by suicide car bombs	27
11 March 2004	Ten near simultaneous bombs are detonated in four commuter trains in Madrid, Spain	191
7 July 2005	Four bombs detonated on three underground trains and a bus in London, United Kingdom	56

Table 7.1 The table above details the major attacks attributed to al Qaeda and related groups since 1996. Many of the attacks were aimed at Western targets in the Middle East and North Africa.

religions is filled with violent images and bloody histories. Sociologist Mark Juergensmeyer explains that "religion deals with the ultimate tension between order and disorder, and disorder is inherently violent, so it is understandable that the chaotic, dangerous character of life is represented in religious images."[128] Symbols and rituals of religious violence, such as bloody conquests in the Muslim and Jewish tradition, sacrificial slaughters of animals, or the violent crucifixion of Christ in Christianity, are common to most religions. In addition, most religions also provide moral and theological justifications for religiously sanctioned violence.

Christian and Jewish doctrine, for example, permits the waging of war and, in certain circumstances, even commands it. In Christianity, a righteous war is referred to as a "just war," while Judaism refers to two forms of war—*Milhemet Hova* and *Milhemet Mitsva*—as religious commandments. In Islam, the doctrine of jihad—a word that means "to strive" or "to exert oneself"—connotes a peaceful as well as a violent struggle.[129]

What then are the roots of religious terrorism, and why has there been a rise in religiously motivated violence in recent decades? Various explanations have been suggested and the answer may be a combination of them.

Terrorism is the tactic of choice for some radical elements within certain religions to protest and, they hope, reverse real or perceived historical injustices. Terrorist tactics embody a source of hope for religious terrorists that they may be able to undo some of their grievances. These grievances may include suppression by a government on religious grounds, the denial of territory that is of religious significance to a group, or a feeling of humiliation on the part of the terrorist. Religious terrorists often start out by feeling humiliated, "enraged that they are viewed by some Other as second class."[130] Believing that their cause is just, and that the population they purport to represent is so deprived, terrorists "persuade themselves that any action—even a heinous crime—is justified."[131]

Also, the use of violence often symbolizes a sense of empowerment, especially to groups that believe that they have been subjected to historical injustices, which are often religious in nature. The sensation of empowerment is especially acute when the enemy is perceived to be militarily or economically stronger.

We must understand not only why extreme elements of religious groups engage in terrorism, but also why there has been an increase in religious terrorism, particularly since the late 1970s. The rise of religious terrorism may be connected to the end of the Cold War between the West and the former Soviet Union. At the end of the Cold War in the late 1980s, old ideologies like communism were discredited. At the same time, economic affluence and civil liberties did not materialize, which led to general feelings of uncertainty. The insecurity has been deepened by other factors, such as high population growth, rapid urbanization, and incapacity on the part of governments to provide basic social services such as medical care and housing.[132] In many countries, religious groups that at times advocate violence have assumed the role of the government in providing these services, thus increasing the popularity of these groups.

The rise of religious terrorism must be understood in the context of modernization. The effects of modernization on traditional societies have been particularly pronounced since the late 1970s. Specifically, religious terrorism may be viewed as the result of the failure of traditional societies to cope with modernization. Some elements within traditional societies may feel "left behind" and channel their anger through violence. More likely, however, is that modernization is viewed as a danger in the eyes of people who are either unwilling or unable to change their traditional habits. In many traditional societies, modernization can be seen as a threat to the traditional way of life. The sexual openness that is taken for granted in the West, for example, may be viewed by others as corrupt and degenerate, and a threat to the more modest roles that women occupy in traditional societies. Westerners are often regarded by religious extremists as people who seek pleasure, rather than people who devote their lives to God or to their families. To the religious majority in traditional societies, modernization poses a threat that modern technologies such as satellite dishes, the Internet, and new transportation systems only accelerate.

RADICAL ISLAMISM

The two final sections of this chapter will be devoted to radical Islamist terrorism, the most acute terrorist threat of our times. As the 9/11 Commission Report states, "the threat posed by Islamist terrorism—especially the al Qaeda network, its affiliates, and its ideology [is the] catastrophic threat at this moment in history." [133] It therefore deserves special mention among the common manifestations of religious terrorism. But what is Islamism and where does it exist? Are all Islamists terrorists, or even all Muslims? What is al Qaeda, how does it operate, and what are its goals?

Whereas Islam is a religion and is therefore in the same class with Judaism and Christianity, Islamism should be understood as an ideology and hence in a class with communism and fascism. Islamism denotes the entrance of Islam into the political sphere in an effort to cope with the problems of modern society. It is important to note that the overwhelming majority of Muslims around the world are not Islamists. Likewise, not all Islamists are terrorists or even advocate terrorism as a legitimate tactic. Hence, while it is difficult to cite precise numbers, keep in mind that radical Islamist terrorists constitute a tiny fraction of all Muslims. Indisputably, the vast majority of Muslims condemn terrorism.

The overarching goal of the Islamist movement is to reshape states in accordance with the conservative formulations of Islamic law, known as the *Sharia*. Islamism comes in various branches, such as Wahhabism, which is dominant in Saudi

Arabia; the Deobandi movement, which established Islamic schools known as *madrassahs* in India, Pakistan, and Afghanistan, from which many militant Islamists are recruited; and the Muslim Brotherhood, which has branches in several Arab and Muslim countries. Each of these branches advocates a puritanical form of Islam and therefore tends to reject democratic principles, wants society to strictly abide by Islamic law, encourages the subservience of women, and warns against the dangers of modernization.

Islamism came into existence in the 1920s, but the latest, and most violent, manifestation of radical Islamism emerged in the aftermath of the 1979 Islamic Revolution in Iran. The Islamic Revolution unseated a secular, pro-American ruler in Iran—Shah Muhammad-Reza Pahlavi—and replaced his regime with one of religious leaders headed by Ayatollah Khomeini. Khomeini embarked on a policy of "Islamization" in Iran, but also hoped to export the Islamic revolution to other countries in the region. While Khomeini's efforts to spread his radical Islamist ideals largely failed in other countries, the revolution in Iran did succeed in inspiring smaller radical movements to fight against "unbelievers" and attempt to establish states ruled on the basis of Islam.

AL QAEDA AND GLOBAL JIHAD

One place to which many of the smaller radical movements flocked soon after the Islamic Revolution was Afghanistan, a country that borders Iran and had been invaded by a military force of "unbelievers" from the Soviet Union. Afghanistan thus attracted many zealous Islamist fighters who hoped to seize upon the momentum of the Islamic Revolution.

One of the persons who helped organize the arrival and training of these foreign fighters was Osama bin Laden, a Saudi national of Yemeni origin and the son of one of Saudi Arabia's richest entrepreneurs. Together with a revered Palestinian Islamic scholar, Abdullah Azzam, bin Laden

Ayatollah Khomeini is shown here in a photograph from 1979. After rising to power in Iran, Khomeini began the process of "Islamization" in Iran, with the hope that his ideology would spread to other nations in the region.

founded the "Services Bureau" (Makhtab al-Khidimat, or MAK) in 1984, which helped finance, train, and recruit radical Islamists to fight the Soviets. The MAK later came to be known as al Qaeda, a terrorist organization and network of groups that has become the embodiment of the threat of radical Islamism and that, over time, has turned into a movement.[134]

Al Qaeda distinguished itself from other terrorist groups by its professionalism. It possessed immense sources of financing, maintained the utmost secrecy, and provided rigorous para-military training. Two characteristics of al Qaeda in particular helped turn it into a professional organization capable of causing immense devastation. First, it was able to use modern technology such as the Internet, e-mail, cell phones, and fax machines more skillfully than any other terrorist group before it. Second, it established a network of fighters in 35 countries, ready and able to perform acts of terrorism. In 2003, the Council on Foreign Relations estimated that autonomous, underground cells affiliated with al Qaeda are present in 100 countries, though the exact extent of al Qaeda's presence is impossible to ascertain.[135] Al Qaeda also established relation-ships with some 30 Islamist terrorist groups, whom it inspired and assisted in attacking national and international targets.

Almost from its inception, al Qaeda has been structured as a network, meaning that unlike traditional "pyramidal" organiza-tions, it has no clear hierarchy. Instead, the network structure consists of so-called cells, groups of up to 15 terrorist operatives who may be tasked with a certain mission. In addition, al Qaeda was organized in such a way that made a centralized leadership unnecessary—it could continue to exist even if one of its "arms" was destroyed.

In February 1998, al Qaeda and a coalition of like-minded affiliated organizations declared jihad against Jews and "Crusaders" (i.e., Christians). Osama bin Laden called upon all Muslims to kill Americans and their allies, including both civilians and military personnel, wherever they were located.

The Arabic word *jihad* means "to strive" or "to exert oneself." In Islam, jihad takes two forms: a peaceful "struggle" against one's evil inclinations (such as the consumption of alcohol), and the struggle of "the sword," which is called for when Islam is perceived to be under attack. Like many other radical Islamists, bin Laden considers the aggressive "jihad of the sword" to be the more important or real jihad.

In the aftermath of the 9/11 attacks, the United States has reportedly killed or captured between 65 percent and 75 percent of al Qaeda's old leadership.[136] However, much of al Qaeda's "first generation" leadership has been replaced by new cadres.

An additional challenge to the United States and other countries threatened by al Qaeda is that the group has morphed from an organization with a clearly identifiable leadership and headquarters to a movement whose members are scattered across the globe and are united by a common idea, namely to fight the "infidels." Al Qaeda regards as infidels all nations who are not abiding by the tenets of Salafism—the strict version of Islam to which al Qaeda's followers subscribe. Its enemies are not only the United States and its close non-Islamic allies in Europe and Israel, but also some Muslim countries in the Middle East. According to al Qaeda, many Arab and Muslim countries, including Saudi Arabia, Egypt, Jordan, and the Gulf States, are heretical despots who are subservient to the United States and are hence to be fought.

In the aftermath of 9/11, the United States invaded Afghanistan and forced the senior leadership of al Qaeda into hiding. As a result, the leadership's ability to plan and direct terrorist attacks has been diminished. Since then, the main threat Osama bin Laden has posed lies in his ability to inspire many Muslims around the world who feel frustrated, alienated, and discriminated against. Osama bin Laden and other radical Islamists have been able to provide many Muslims who feel victimized and exploited with a sense of empowerment, which in turn spurred the desire to exact revenge on the despised foes.

The transnational movement that formed in the aftermath of the 9/11 attacks is best understood as a global jihad movement. The term "global jihad movement" is a more accurate description than "al Qaeda" for the danger confronting the United States and other countries at present and in the foreseeable future. It consists of a large network of like-minded groups that are united by a common desire to wage holy war on all infidels. Their aim is to establish a caliphate—the Muslim world's traditional system of governance—in all countries that have ever been under Muslim domination. Global jihadis are present in most countries of the world today, and they are able to organize themselves in small cells, with little or no connection to the remnants of al Qaeda's senior leadership, who are believed to hide in the region along the Afghan-Pakistani border.

The rapid rise of the global jihad movement is also a result of the Internet and other modern systems of communication and information such as faxes, cell phones, and laptops. The Internet allows young and alienated Muslims, wherever they may be, to link up with other members of a virtual Islamic community of like-minded individuals who, whether justified or not, have a long list of grievances against the United States. If members of this virtual community are serious about inflicting harm on the United States or other countries, they are able to learn the tricks of the terrorism trade from readily available sources on the World Wide Web, including Websites that teach aspiring jihadis how to build bombs or how to wage a guerrilla war. The global jihad movement is therefore a function and product of the information and globalization age.

In March 2003, the United States led a coalition that invaded Iraq and removed from power Saddam Hussein, a brutal dictator responsible for the killing of hundreds of thousands of innocent Iraqi citizens. The presence of U.S. forces in Iraq, however, has had the negative side effect of motivating many young Muslims to travel to Iraq and volunteer for what they call a jihad against the heretical occupier of Muslim lands. The war against Iraq has prompted a protracted guerrilla and terrorist insurgency that, at the time of this writing, has resulted in the killing of thousands of coalition armed servicemen and women, as well as Iraqi soldiers and policemen. Some 4,000 people have been killed in terrorist bombings. Altogether, tens of thousands of Iraqi civilians have lost their lives as a result of war, terrorism, and crime since Saddam Hussein's removal from power.[137]

The Iraq war has demonstrated the relative ease with which the global jihad movement, of which al Qaeda is still the nominal head, grows. In October 2004, the most notorious terrorist mastermind active in Iraq after the U.S. invasion, Abu Musab al-Zarqawi, swore allegiance to Osama bin Laden, and subsequently changed the name of his terrorist organization from *Al-Tawhid w'al Jihad* (Unity and Jihad) to "Al Qaeda in the Land of the Two Rivers," referring to the Iraqi rivers Euphrates and Tigris. The global jihad movement has inspired other terrorist cells to perpetrate terrorist attacks worldwide, including suicide and other bombings in Morocco, Turkey, Madrid, and London. The global jihad movement is likely to remain the predominant threat to Western countries and many Arab and Muslim regimes for at least a generation.

SUMMARY

Religious terrorism has been part of the tradition of all major religions, including Judaism, Christianity, Islam, and Hinduism. Part of the reason that almost every religion has produced violent elements is that religion itself is an ambiguous phenomenon. While religions are often associated with positive values such as peace and compassion, all major religions have also justified violence and wars under certain circumstances.

The roots of religious terrorism are complex: We find them in the real or perceived grievances of societies as well as in the psychological needs of those communities. They are also tied to political developments—such as the collapse of communism and the Islamic Revolution—that boost religiosity in general and violence in the name of religion. Finally, religious terrorism can be traced to the profound changes introduced by modernity.

Radical Islamist terrorism is likely to remain the dominant security threat to the West and to moderate Arab and Muslim states in the near future. However, it is important to note that only a tiny, radical fringe among Muslims condones violence. It is also important to separate Islam, which above all preaches peace, from radical Islamism, a political ideology that has hijacked the religion of Islam to justify the use of violence for its political goals.

CHAPTER 8

CONCLUSION

This book examined the causes of terrorism from three interrelated perspectives. At the level of the individual terrorist, we focused on individual psychology, including the mental state of the terrorist, his psychological justifications to engage in violence, and his interactions with the terrorist group. At the level of the terrorist organization, we examined organizational goals and motives to engage in terrorism. Finally, the environmental perspective focused on social, political, economic, cultural, historical, and religious conditions that give rise to terrorism.

Too often, terrorism is explained from only one of these perspectives. Officials of governments affected by terrorism tend to focus on the individual level, often neglecting important environmental

A Russian police officer carries a baby released by Chechen militants, above. In 2004, Chechen terrorists invaded a Russian school, taking hundreds of schoolchildren and adults hostage. Over the course of the multi-day seige, approximately 344 civilians were killed, including over 170 children.

conditions that help to breed terrorism. Government leaders often dehumanize terrorists by calling them "monsters"; label them as deranged; or simply insult them, as Russian president Vladimir Putin did when he called Chechen terrorists "bastards" in response to a school massacre in the town of Beslan in 2004.[138] While such statements can be emotionally satisfying, they fail to take into account environmental conditions that create terrorists' grievances. Viewing Chechen, Basque, or Palestinian terrorists as morally depraved—as many Russian, Spanish, or Israeli leaders do—without trying to understand the economic, political, and social context from which the terrorists operate, helps leaders avoid having to attend to the grievances of these societies.

Equally flawed are explanations that focus solely on environmental conditions. Those advancing these explanations claim that groups and individuals engage in terrorism simply because the environment in which terrorists find themselves leaves them no other choice. Such explanations tend to be sympathetic toward terrorists, at times going as far as arguing that those who engage in terrorism are innocent and desperate victims driven into violence by intolerable circumstances. While it is certainly correct to identify humiliation and desperation as a major contributing factor to the formation of a culture of suicide bombing, one must not ignore the culpability on the part of the individual terrorists and their organizations. Terrorists should be held morally and legally accountable for their deeds. More importantly, arguments that stress the role of the environment in creating terrorists while neglecting the role of the individual do not explain why most people who live under dire economic and political conditions do not resort to terrorism. What seems to lie at the roots of terrorism is how an individual terrorist *perceives* the injustice, which affects the amount of anger and frustration that a supposed injustice will generate.

In order to avoid simplistic and unsatisfying explanations of terrorism, this book has adopted a multi-causal view that explains terrorism as the result of an interaction between individual (psychological), organizational, and environmental factors. To understand the causes of terrorism, the motives of the individual terrorist are as important as the goals of the terrorist organization. Both the individual and the organization, in turn, are influenced by the environmental conditions that surround them.

As far as the individual terrorist is concerned, most psychologists and terrorism analysts have concluded that terrorists are not mentally ill. Terrorists are mostly normal people who may have an above-normal tendency to seek excitement and adventures. The precise motivations of each individual for joining the terrorist group and executing an attack are impossible to delineate. As one former State Department official put it, "there are probably as many reasons for committing terrorist acts as there are terrorists."[139] It is more plausible to assume that terrorists are motivated by several factors at once. There are a number of possible risk factors that may increase the likelihood of terrorism in a particular setting.[140] These include:

- socio-economic risk factors such as poverty, a high unemployment rate, slow economic growth, and relative deprivation;

- political risk factors such as government repression, denial of basic rights, foreign occupation, or "weak states" that are unable to provide basic services and control their territory;

- cultural and historical risk factors such as a historical tendency for violent resistance to foreign intrusion or traumatic experiences with oppression and even genocide;

- and religious risk factors such as the denial of a territory that has a high religious significance to a group.

To be sure, none of these risk factors directly causes terrorism. Poverty does not directly affect terrorism and, as we have seen, poor people are not more likely to engage in terrorism than their wealthier counterparts. However, poverty may have indirect effects by creating weak states where government control is weak, allowing terrorist organizations to establish a safe haven. While none of these individual risk factors in isolation lead to terrorism, it is plausible that where a large number of these risk factors coincide, terrorism is more likely to occur.

The organizational analysis of terrorism is a crucial one, because the overwhelming majority of terrorist activities are organized and executed by members of organizations. Their abhorrent methods and lack of remorse notwithstanding, these organizations should be considered as acting rationally because they possess sets of values, beliefs, and images of the larger environment that are internally consistent. They also see terrorism as a logical means to achieving the goals they desire.[141]

The basic goal of the terrorist organization is to guarantee its own survival. Terrorists would lose much if their organization ceased to exist, as terrorist groups provide their members with a sense of belonging and a place to form and strengthen social bonds. Terrorist organizations also often imbue their members with social status, empowerment, and financial rewards. The destruction of the terrorist group would entail an end to these material and immaterial rewards.

An additional reason for organizations to adopt terrorism in general, or a particular tactic such as suicide bombings, can be rivalry with other groups for power. Terrorist organizations may believe that suicide bombings, for example, will help increase public support in locations where a large portion of the population openly supports this tactic.[142] Terrorist organizations are also likely to be influenced by a number of strategic and tactical calculations. Organizations may consider a particular time or opportunity to be likely to lead to success, or they may believe that the costs of failure are low. Organizations can also be influenced by the successes and failures of other terrorist organizations, adapting their tactics accordingly.

By virtue of its nature as a group, the terrorist organization fulfills some of the psychological needs that are likely to have played a role in the individual's joining the group. Once he becomes a member, the individual undergoes a psychological transformation that results in his or her assumption of a new identity as a group member, rather than as an individual. Maintaining that new identity, which in turn satisfies such

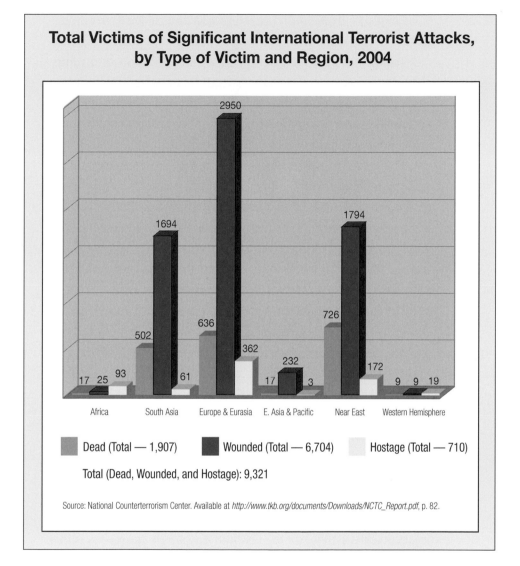

Total Victims of Significant International Terrorist Attacks, by Type of Victim and Region, 2004

Africa: 17, 25, 93
South Asia: 502, 1694, 61
Europe & Eurasia: 636, 2950, 362
E. Asia & Pacific: 17, 232, 3
Near East: 726, 1794, 172
Western Hemisphere: 9, 9, 19

Dead (Total — 1,907)   Wounded (Total — 6,704)   Hostage (Total — 710)

Total (Dead, Wounded, and Hostage): 9,321

Source: National Counterterrorism Center. Available at *http://www.tkb.org/documents/Downloads/NCTC_Report.pdf*, p. 82.

Table 8.1 **This table from the National Counterterrorism Center shows that people wounded in terrorist attacks outnumber those who are killed or taken hostage. In 2004, there were more victims of terrorist attacks in Europe and Eurasia than in any other region.**

needs as a sense of belonging, helps to empower the individual. Remaining a member of this group may even become a more important goal than participation in an act of terrorism.

Finally, both the individual terrorist and the terrorist organization are influenced by environmental factors. Environmental risk factors that are likely to influence the decision of an individual to join a terrorist group also affect the organization. Like individuals, organizations see their environment through a certain lens, and *perception* of environment, rather than an objective reality, ultimately influences the organization's decisions.

The perceptions of the organization are reflected in the guiding ideology. An ideology captures the view that a particular group has of the world as it exists and as it ought to be, according to that ideology. An ideology also can provide clues about what its most fervent supporters might be willing to do to change the existing world. For example, anybody who had read Adolf Hitler's book *Mein Kampf* before the National Socialists' seizure of power in Germany should not have been surprised that the Nazi regime aggressively expanded its territory or exterminated peoples believed to be inferior to their own "Aryan master race." [143]

Terrorist organizations that subscribe to various ideologies, be they Islamism, communism, or fascism, each in their own way use these ideologies to rationalize the use of violence. This is where the danger of ideology lies, and we would be well advised to pay close attention to the ideologies that terrorist organizations espouse.

Terrorism, we can conclude, has multiple roots. Recognizing that terrorism is not the result of any single cause, but rather the product of a highly complex interplay of different factors—individual psychology, organizational, and environmental factors—is important because it helps governments design more effective responses. For governments, the knowledge that there is no single cause of terrorism could help them refrain from single solutions that are all but certain to fail. Military crackdowns on organizations, for instance—necessary as they are in some cases—may help reduce terrorism in the short term by neutralizing those who execute the attacks, but they may also exacerbate political, economic, and social risk factors in the long run.

Effective counter-terrorism must consist of several approaches, including reducing the grievances and other risk factors; limiting the ability of terrorist organizations to conduct attacks; physically "hardening" the facilities that are at high risk of attack; creating and maintaining effective intelligence services to detect terrorist threats in advance; and engaging in public diplomacy that is generally respectful of other nations and cultures.

Unfortunately, even if states take all of these counter-measures, terrorism is unlikely to disappear altogether. Terrorism has existed for millennia, and people will almost certainly continue to perceive their realities in ways that lead them to conclude that violence is the best means to achieve their goals. The United States and other countries affected by terrorism should therefore be as prepared as possible to face a threat that will accompany us into the future. Curbing terrorism wherever and whenever possible, rather than the unrealistic goal of eliminating terrorism altogether, should be the primary objective. Understanding its roots, however, must be the first step.

Chapter 1
What Is Terrorism?

1. See Anonymous, *Imperial Hubris: Why the West Is Losing the War on Terror.* Washington, D.C.: Brassey's, 2004.

2. Bruce Hoffman, *Inside Terrorism.* New York: Columbia University Press, 1998, pp. 14–15.

3. This definition contains elements of the one used by the U.S. State Department, which defines terrorism as "premeditated, politically motivated violence perpetrated against noncombatant targets by subnational groups or clandestine agents, usually intended to influence an audience"; and elements of the definition used by Bruce Hoffman: "The deliberate creation and exploitation of fear through violence or the threat of violence in the pursuit of political change." See Hoffman, *Inside Terrorism*, p. 43. Noncombatants include both civilians as well as military personnel who are unarmed and/or not on duty. See U.S. Department of State, *Patterns of Global Terrorism 2003*, p. xii. Available online at http://www.state.gov/s/ct/rls/pgtrpt/2003.

4. Michael T. Kaufman, "Idi Amin, Murderous and Erratic Ruler of Uganda in the 70's, Dies in Exile," *New York Times* (August 17, 2003), p. 32.

5. Paul Pillar, *Terrorism and U.S. Foreign Policy.* Washington, D.C.: Brookings Institution, 2001, pp. 19–29.

6. Ibid., p. 27.

7. On the specter of nuclear terrorism, see Graham Allison, *Nuclear Terrorism: The Ultimate Preventable Catastrophe.* New York: Times Books/Henry Holt, 2004.

8. See Assaf Moghadam, *A Global Resurgence of Religion?* Cambridge, MA: Weatherhead Center for International Affairs, 2003. Available online at http://www.wcfia.harvard.edu/papers/723__Moghadam03_03.pdf.

9. Several scholars have recognized the need for terrorism analysis on these three levels. See Martha Crenshaw, "The Causes of Terrorism," *Comparative Politics* 13:4 (July 1981): pp. 379–399. Jacob M. Rabbie, "A Behavioral Interaction Model: Toward a Social-Psychological Framework for Studying Terrorism," *Terrorism and Political Violence* 3:4 (Winter 1991): pp. 134–163. Donatella della Porta, *Social Movements, Political Violence, and the State: A Comparative Analysis of Italy and Germany.* Cambridge, UK: Cambridge University Press, 1995.

Chapter 2
Psychological Explanations of Terrorism

10. Jeff Victoroff, "The Mind of the Terrorist: A Review and Critique of Psychological Approaches," *Journal of Conflict Resolution* 49:1 (February 2005): pp. 12–13.

11. Ibid., p. 17.

12. Marc Sageman, *Understanding Terror Networks.* Philadelphia: University of Pennsylvania Press, 2004, p. 83.

13. See Crenshaw, "The Causes of Terrorism," pp. 379–399. C.R. McCauley and M.E. Segal, "Social Psychology of Terrorist Groups," in C. Hendrick, et al., *Group Processes and Intergroup Relations*, Vol. 9 of *Annual Review of Social and Personality Psychology.* Beverly Hills, CA: Sage, 1987.

14. Compare Jessica Stern, *The Ultimate Terrorists.* Cambridge, MA: Harvard University Press, 1999, p. 77.

15. Rex A. Hudson, "The Sociology and Psychology of Terrorism: Who Becomes a Terrorist and Why?" Library of Congress, Federal Research Division (September 1999), p. 27. Available online at http://www.loc.gov/rr/frd/pdf-files/Soc_Psych_of_Terrorism.pdf.

16. Victoroff, "The Mind of the Terrorist," pp. 3–42.

17. On identity theory, see Peter A. Olsson, "The Terrorist and the Terrorized: Some Psychoanalytic Considerations," *Journal of Psychohistory* 16:1 (1988): pp. 47–60. Maxwell Taylor and Ethel Quayle, *Terrorist Lives.* New York: Brassey's, 1994.

18. On narcissism theory, see Heinz Kohut, "Thoughts on Narcissism and Narcissistic Rage," *Psychoanalytic Study of the Child* 27 (1972): pp. 360–400. Heinz Kohut, *The Search for the Self.* New York: International Universities Press, 1978. J.W. Crayton, "Terrorism and Psychology of the Self," in Lawrence Z. Freedman and Yonah Alexander, eds., *Perspectives on Terrorism.* Wilmington, DE: Scholarly Resources, 1983, pp. 3341.

19. Jerrold M. Post, "Terrorist Psycho-Logic: Terrorist Behavior as a Product of Psychological Forces," in Walter Reich, ed., *Origins of Terrorism: Psychologies, Ideologies, Theologies, States of Mind.* Washington, D.C.: Woodrow Wilson Center Press, 1998, p. 27.

20. Ibid., p. 25.

21. Robert S. Robins and Jerrold M. Post, *Political Paranoia: The Psychopolitics of Hatred.* New Haven, CT: Yale University Press, 1997.

22. Victoroff, "The Mind of the Terrorist," pp. 28–29.

23. Ibid., p. 26.

24. See Mark Juergensmeyer, *Terror in the Mind of God: The Global Rise of Religious Violence.* Berkeley, CA: University of California Press, 2001. Eyad al-Sarraj, "Suicide Bombers: Dignity, Despair, and the Need of Hope," *Journal of Palestine Studies* 124 (Summer 2002). Hilal Khashan, "Collective Palestinian Frustration and Suicide Bombings," *Third World Quarterly* 24:6. Jessica Stern, *Terror in the Name of God: Why Religious Militants Kill.* New York: Ecco/Harper Collins, 2003.

25. Victoroff, "The Mind of the Terrorist," p. 29.

26. Quoted in Ehud Sprinzak, "Rational Fanatics," *Foreign Policy* (September/October 2000), p. 68.

27. Albert Bandura, "Mechanisms of Moral Disengagement," in Reich, *Origins of Terrorism,* p. 181.

28. For a discussion on brainwashing, see Robert Jay Lifton, *Thought Reform and the Psychology of Totalism: A Study of 'Brainwashing' in China.* New York: Norton, 1961.

29. Irving L. Janis, *Victims of Groupthink: A Psychological Study of Foreign-Policy Decisions and Fiascoes.* Boston: Houghton Mifflin, 1972.

30. For an in-depth discussion of Aum Shinrikyo and brainwashing, see Robert Jay Lifton, *Destroying the World to Save It.* New York: Owl Books, 1999.

31. Crenshaw, "The Causes of Terrorism," p. 390.

32. See Walter Reich, "Understanding Terrorist Behavior: The Limits and Opportunities of Psychological Inquiry," in Reich, *Origins of Terrorism,* pp. 261–279. On the sociological neglect of envy, see Paul Wilkinson, "Social Scientific Theory and Civil Violence," in Yonah Alexander, David Carlton, and Paul Wilkinson, eds., *Terrorism: Theory and Practice.* Boulder, CO: Westview Press, 1979, p. 58.

Chapter 3
Organizational Explanations of Terrorism

33. Martha Crenshaw, "The Psychology of Terrorism: An Agenda for the 21st Century," *Political Psychology* 21:2 (2000): p. 409.

34. The theoretical content of this chapter is based largely on two articles by Martha Crenshaw, who first formulated the organizational approach to

terrorism. See Martha Crenshaw, "An Organizational Approach to the Analysis of Political Terrorism," *Orbis* 29 (Fall 1985), pp. 465–489. Martha Crenshaw, "Theories of Terrorism: Instrumental and Organizational Approaches," in David C. Rapoport, ed., *Inside Terrorist Organizations.* New York: Frank Cass, 1988, pp. 44–62.

35. See Assaf Moghadam, "Palestinian Suicide Terrorism in the Second Intifada: Motivations and Organizational Aspects," *Studies in Conflict and Terrorism* 26:2 (March/April 2003): p. 68.

36. Chester I. Barnard, *The Functions of the Executive.* Cambridge, MA: Harvard University Press, 1938, p. 216. James Q. Wilson, *Political Organizations.* New York: Basic Books, 1973, pp. 30–36.

37. Walter Laqueur, *The Age of Terrorism.* Boston: Little, Brown, 1987, p. 96.

38. Mia M. Bloom, *Dying to Kill: The Allure of Suicide Terror.* New York: Columbia University Press, 2005.

39. Martha Crenshaw, "The Logic of Terrorism: Terrorist Behavior as a Product of Strategic Choice," in Reich, *Origins of Terrorism*, pp. 7–24.

40. Ehud Sprinzak, "The Psychological Formation of Extreme Left Terrorism in a Democracy: The Case of the Weathermen," in Reich, *Origins of Terrorism*, pp. 65–85.

41. Compare Martha Crenshaw, "Theories of Terrorism: Instrumental and Organizational Approaches," in Rapoport, *Inside Terrorist Organizations,* pp. 44–62.

42. Martha Crenshaw, ed., *Terrorism, Legitimacy and Power.* Middletown, CT: Wesleyan University Press, p. 17. Quoted in Brynjar Lia and Katja H.-W. Skjølberg, "Why Terrorism Occurs: A Survey of Theories and Hypotheses on the Causes of Terrorism," Norwegian Defence Research Establishment (May 30, 2000), p. 14.

43. See Assaf Moghadam, "Suicide Bombings in the Israeli-Palestinian Conflict: A Conceptual Framework," *Project for the Research of Islamist Movements (PRISM)* (May 2002), pp. 65–68. Available online at http://www.e-prism.org.

44. Quoted in Burhan Wazir, "Suicide Bombing is Democratic Right, Says the 'Soul' of Hamas," *The Observer* (August 19, 2001), p. 20.

45. Quoted in Yonah Alexander, "Terrorism and the Media: Some Considerations," in Alexander, *Terrorism: Theory and Practice,* p. 160.

46. Former British prime minister Margaret Thatcher, quoted in Hoffman, *Inside Terrorism*, p. 143.

47. Ibid., p. 142.

48. Compare Paul Wilkinson, "The Media and Terrorism: A Reassessment," *Terrorism and Political Violence* 9:2 (Summer 1997).

Chapter 4
Political Explanations of Terrorism

49. Hoffman, *Inside Terrorism*, p. 14.

50. Robert Friedlander argues that modern political science tends to treat assassination as an act of terrorism. See Robert Friedlander, *Terrorism: Documents of International and Local Control.* Dobbs Ferry, NY: Oceana, 1979, p. 7. Bruce Hoffman, in contrast, argues that "to qualify as terrorism, violence must be perpetrated by some organizational entity with at least some conspiratorial structure and identifiable chain of command beyond a single individual acting on his or her own." Hoffman, *Inside Terrorism*, pp. 42–43.

51. Alex P. Schmid, "The Problems of Defining Terrorism," in Martha Crenshaw and John Pimlott, eds., *Encyclopedia of World Terrorism, Vol. 1.* Armonk, NY: Sharpe Reference, 1997, pp. 12–14.

52. Laqueur, *The Age of Terrorism*, pp. 15–17.

53. Hoffman, *Inside Terrorism*, p. 24.

54. Ian O. Lesser, "Introduction," in Ian O. Lesser et al., *Countering the New Terrorism*. Santa Monica, CA: RAND, 1999, p. 1.

55. See Peter Merkl, "West German Left-Wing Terrorism," in Martha Crenshaw, ed., *Terrorism in Context*. University Park, PA: Pennsylvania State University Press, 1995, pp. 160–210.

56. Donatella Della Porta, "Left-Wing Terrorism in Italy," in Crenshaw, *Terrorism in Context*, pp. 105–159.

57. Hoffman, *Inside Terrorism*, p. 165.

58. Ibid., p. 186.

59. See Amos Harel, "Hezbollah's Terror Factory in the PA," *Haaretz* (January 11, 2005). Kathryn Westcott, "Who are Hezbollah?" *BBC News Online* (April 4, 2002), available online at http://news.bbc.co.uk/2/hi/middle east/1908671.stm.

60. For an overview of the centrality of power in national and international politics, and in the study of political science and international relations, see James E. Dougherty and Robert L. Pfaltzgraff, Jr., *Contending Theories of International Relations: A Comprehensive Survey*, 5th Edition. New York: Longman, 2001, pp. 16, 54 (footnotes 53–54).

61. Ibid., pp. 14–15.

62. Zeev Schiff and Ehud Yaari, *Intifada-The Palestinian Uprising: Israel's Third Front*. New York: Simon and Schuster, 1989, p. 91.

63. Ibid., pp. 82–83.

64. Crenshaw, "The Causes of Terrorism," p. 385.

65. Ibid., pp. 394.

66. Paul Wilkinson, *Political Terrorism*. New York: John Wiley & Sons, 1972, pp. 108–109.

67. On how ineffective governments are particularly at risk of suffering from terrorism and insurgency, see Crenshaw, "The Causes of Terrorism." Paul Collier, "Economic Causes of Civil Conflict and their Implications for Policy," *World Bank Paper* (June 15, 2000). James Fearon and David Laitin, "Ethnicity, Insurgency, and Civil War," *American Political Science Review* 97:1 (January 2003): pp. 75–90. On weak states, see Robert I. Rotberg, ed., *When States Fail: Causes and Consequences*. Princeton, NJ: Princeton University Press, 2004. William Zartman, *Collapsed States*. Boulder, CO: Lynne Rienner, 1995. Donald Snow, *Uncivil Wars: International Security and the New Internal Conflicts*. Boulder, CO: Lynne Rienner, 1996.

68. C.J.M. Drake, "The Role of Ideology in Terrorists' Target Selection," *Terrorism and Political Violence* 10:2 (Summer 1998).

69. Martin Seliger, *Ideology and Politics*. New York: Free Press, 1976.

Chapter 5
The Role of Economics, Modernization, and Globalization

70. Radio Address by the President to the Nation (November 10, 2001). Available online at http://www.whitehouse.gov/news/releases/2001/11/20011110.html.

71. Quoted in Janet J. Jai, "Getting at the Roots of Terrorism," *Christian Science Monitor* (December 10, 2001).

72. Ibid.

73. Charles Russell and Bowman Miller, "Profile of a Terrorist," in Lawrence Z. Freedman and Yonah Alexander, eds., *Perspectives of Terrorism*. Wilmington, DE: Scholarly Resources, 1983, pp. 45–60.

74. Walter Laqueur, *No End to War: Terrorism in the 21st Century*. New York: Continuum, 2004, p. 15.

75. The poll was conducted by the Palestinian Center for Policy and Survey Research. See Alan B. Krueger and Jitka Maleckova, "Education, Poverty, Political Violence and Terrorism: Is There a Causal Connection?" NBER Working Paper No. 9074 (July 2002), pp. 13–19.

76. For surveys on Palestinian support for terrorism, see the website of the Jerusalem Media and Communication Centre (JMCC), available at http://www.jmcc.org/.

77. Krueger and Maleckova, "Education, Poverty, Political Violence and Terrorism," pp. 13–19. See also James A. Piazza, "Rooted in Poverty? Terrorism, Poor Economic Development and Social Cleavages," *Terrorism and Political Violence* (Spring 2005). Alberto Abadie, "Poverty, Political Freedom, and the Roots of Terrorism," NBER Working Paper No. w10859 (October 2004).

78. Michael Radu, "The Futile Search for Root Causes of Terrorism," Foreign Policy Research Institute (FPRI) E-Note (April 23, 2002). Available online at http://www.fpri.org/enotes/americawar.20020423.radu.futilesearchforrootcauses.html

79. On Sudan, see *The 9/11 Commission Report: Final Report of the National Commission on Terrorist Attacks Upon the United States*, Authorized Edition. New York: W.W. Norton, 2004, p. 57. On Afghanistan, see *The 9/11 Commission Report*, p. 66.

80. See James D. Fearon and David D. Laitin, "Ethnicity, Insurgency, and Civil War." Paul Collier and Anke Hoeffler, "On the Economic Causes of Civil War," *Oxford Economic Papers* 50:4 (1998), pp. 563–573.

81. Robert J. Barro, "Inequality, Growth, and Investment," NBER Working Paper w7038 (March 1999).

82. *Arab Human Development Report 2003*. New York: United Nations Development Programme, 2003, p. 137.

83. Paul Collier, "Economic Causes of Civil Conflict and their Implications for Policy," *World Bank Paper* (June 15, 2000), p. 2. Available online at http://www.worldbank.org/research/conflict/papers/civilconflict.pdf.

84. U.S. Department of State, *Patterns of Global Terrorism 2003*, p. 133.

85. Collier, "Economic Causes of Civil Conflict and Their Implications for Policy," p. 4.

86. Jessica Stern, *Terror in the Name of God: Why Religious Militants Kill*. New York: Ecco/Harper Collins, 2003, p. 189.

87. Ibid., p. 216.

88. Moghadam, "Palestinian Suicide Terrorism in the Second Intifada," p. 73.

89. Bill Keller, "Springtime for Saddam," *New York Times* (April 6, 2002), A15.

90. See Samuel Huntington, *Political Order in Changing Societies*. New Haven, CT: Yale University Press, 1968.

91. Thomas L. Friedman, *The Lexus and the Olive Tree*, 2nd edition. New York: Anchor Books, 2000, p. 9.

92. "Mapping the Global Future," Report of the National Intelligence Council's 2020 Project Based on Consultations with Nongovernmental Experts Around the World (December 2004), p. 10. Available online at http://www.foia.cia.gov/2020/2020.pdf.

93. For a critical view of globalization, see Mary Kaldor, *New and Old Wars: Organized Violence in a Global Era*. Stanford, CA: Stanford University Press, 1999, especially Chapter 4. On the clash between global capitalism and traditional tribalism, see Benjamin R. Barber, *Jihad vs. McWorld*. New York: Ballantine Books, 1996.

94. Quan Li and Drew Schaub, "Economic Globalization and Transnational Terrorism: A Pooled Time-Series Analysis," *Journal of Conflict Resolution* 48:2 (April 2004): pp. 230–258.

95. See Michael J. Stevens, "The Unanticipated Consequences of Globalization: Contextualizing Terrorism," in Chris Stout, ed., *The Psychology of Terrorism, Vol. 3: Theoretical Understandings and Perspectives.* Westport, CT: Praeger, 2002, pp. 31–56.

96. Ibid., p. 34.

97. For more on network organizations and network-based warfare, see John Arquilla and David Ronfeldt, *Networks and Netwars: The Future of Terror, Crime, and Militancy.* Santa Monica, CA: RAND, 2001. Marc Sageman, *Understanding Terror Networks.* Philadelphia: University of Pennsylvania Press, 2004.

98. Council on Foreign Relations, "Al Qaeda," *Terrorism Questions & Answers.* Available online at http://www.terrorismanswers.org/ groups/alqaeda.html.

99. On steganography, see Jack Kelley, "Terror Groups Hide Behind Web Encryption," *USA Today* (February 5, 2001). Declan McCullagh, "Bin Laden: Steganography Master?" *Wired News* (February 7, 2001).

100. Hendrik Hertzberg, "Tuesday and After," *The New Yorker* (September 24, 2001), p. 27.

Chapter 6
Society, Culture, and Terrorism

101. Ingo Butters, Cordula Meyer, and Caroline Schmidt, "Das Nest der Schläfer," *Der Spiegel* Internet Edition (September 14, 2001).

102. Charles Russell and Bowman Miller, "Profile of a Terrorist," *Terrorism: An International Journal* 1:1 (1977): pp. 17–34.

103. Amy Waldman, "Sri Lanka's Young are Forced to Fill Ranks of Endless Rebellion," *New York Times* (January 6, 2003).

104. Hudson, "The Sociology and Psychology of Terrorism," pp. 41–43.

105. Matthew Guttman, "The Bomber Next Door," *Jerusalem Post* (September 14, 2001), 5B.

106. Council on Foreign Relations, "Terrorist, Guerrilla, Freedom Fighter: What's the Difference?" Terrorism Questions & Answers. Available online at http://www.cfrterrorism.org/policy/ guerrilla.html.

107. Fernando Reinares, "Who are the Terrorists? Analyzing Changes in Sociological Profile Among Members of ETA," *Studies in Conflict and Terrorism* 27:6 (November/December 2004): pp. 466–467.

108. Johan Galtung, "Violence, Peace and Peace Research," *Journal of Peace Research* 6:3 (1969): pp. 167–191.

109. Government of Rwanda Genocide Census: "Denombrement des Victimes du Genocide," Ministere de l'Administration Locale et des Affaires Sociales (March 2001). Human Rights Watch estimates that approximately 500,000 Tutsis were killed during that period.

110. Ted Robert Gurr, *Why Men Rebel.* Princeton, NJ: Princeton University Press, 1970.

111. Scott Atran, "Mishandling Suicide Terrorism," *Washington Quarterly* (Summer 2004), p. 78.

112. See Dennis A. Pluchinsky, "Terrorism in the Former Soviet Union: A Primer, a Puzzle, a Prognosis," *Studies in Conflict and Terrorism* 21:2 (April-June 1998): pp. 119–148.

113. See Giovanni Caracci, "Cultural and Contextual Aspects of Terrorism," in Stout, *The Psychology of Terrorism,* pp. 58–60. Caracci identifies more than five cultural/contextual issues underlying terrorist activity.

114. Russian authorities have refused to publicize the exact number of Russian soldiers killed and wounded in the campaigns against Chechnya. For estimates, see Boris Sapozhnikov, "Second Chechen Campaign Takes its Toll," *Gazeta* (February 18, 2003). Published online by the Center for Defense Information (CDI), available at http://www.cdi.org/russia/johnson/7067-8.cfm.

115. Moghadam, "Suicide Bombings in the Israeli-Palestinian Conflict: A Conceptual Framework," pp. 36–38.

116. Caracci, "Cultural and Contextual Aspects of Terrorism," pp. 63–64.

117. The Pew Research Center for the People and the Press, "Views of a Changing World" (June 2003). Available online at http://people-press.org/reports/pdf/185.pdf.

118. On the importance of narratives, see Marc Howard Ross, "The Political Psychology of Competing Narratives: September 11 and Beyond," in Craig Calhoun, Paul Price, and Ashley Timmer, eds., *Understanding September 11.* New York: The New Press, 2002, p. 303.

119. See Khachig Tololyan, "Cultural Narrative and the Motivation of the Terrorist," in David C. Rapoport, ed., *Inside Terrorist Organizations.* New York: Columbia University Press, 1988, pp. 218–221.

120. For a legal definition of the term *genocide*, see "Convention on the Prevention and Punishment of the Crime of Genocide," Office of the High Commissioner for Human Rights, United Nations. Available online at http://www.unhchr.ch/html/menu3/b/p_genoci.htm.

121. See Joseph V. Montville, "Psychoanalytic Enlightenment and the Greening of Diplomacy," in Vamik D. Volkan, Joseph V. Montville, and Demetrios A. Julius, *The Psychodynamics of International Relationships.* Lexington, MA: Lexington Books, 1991, p. 180.

122. Tololyan, "Cultural Narrative and the Motivation of the Terrorist," p. 231.

Chapter 7
Religious Explanations of Terrorism

123. Hoffman, *Inside Terrorism*, pp. 93–94.

124. For a list of organizations and individuals designated as terrorist entities, see U.S. Department of State, *Patterns of Global Terrorism 2003.* Available online at http://www.state.gov/s/ct/rls/pgtrpt.

125. Compare David C. Rapoport, "Fear and Trembling: Terrorism in Three Religious Traditions," *American Political Science Review* 78:3 (September 1984): p. 659. Rapoport goes as far as arguing that prior to the 18th century, religion was the only justification for terrorism.

126. On how religious terrorists perceive their struggles in grand terms of "good vs. evil," see Mark Juergensmeyer, *Terror in the Mind of God: The Global Rise of Religious Violence.* Berkeley, CA: University of California Press, 2001, pp. 145–163.

127. For a discussion of demands made by al Qaeda, see the arguments of former CIA analyst Michael Scheuer in Anonymous, *Imperial Hubris: Why the West is Losing the War on Terror.* Washington, D.C.: Brassey's, 2004, pp. xv–19.

128. Mark Juergensmeyer, "The Logic of Religious Violence," in Russell D. Howard and Reid L. Sawyer, *Terrorism and Counterterrorism: Understanding the New Security Environment.* Guilford, CT: McGraw-Hill, 2003, p. 143.

129. For more on the connection between religion and violence, see Marc Gopin, *Between Eden and Armaggedon: The Future of World Religions, Violence, and Peacemaking.* New York: Oxford University Press, 2000. R. Scott Appleby, *The Ambivalence of the Sacred: Religion, Violence, and Reconciliation.* Lanham, MD: Rowman & Littlefield, 2000.

130. Stern, *Terror in the Name of God*, p. 282.

131. Ibid.

132. Hoffman, *Inside Terrorism*, p. 92.

133. See *The 9/11 Commission Report*, p. 362.

134. For the evolution of al Qaeda, see Anonymous, *Through Our Enemies' Eyes*. Washington, D.C.: Brassey's, 2003. See also Rohan Gunaratna, *Inside Al Qaeda: Global Network of Terror*. New York: Columbia University Press, 2002. Jason Burke, *Al Qaeda: Casting a Shadow of Terror*. New York: I.B. Tauris, 2003.

135. Council on Foreign Relations, "Al Qaeda," Terrorism Questions & Answers. Available online at http://www.terrorismanswers.org.

136. See "Fact-Checking the Debate: Analyzing the Statements of President Bush and Senator John Kerry," *Boston Globe* (October 1, 2004). Available online at http://www.boston.com/news/politics/debates/articles/2004/10/01/debatefacts.

137. All data on casualties in Iraq is taken from the Brookings Institution's *Iraq Index*. Available online at http://www.brookings.edu/fp/saban/iraq/index.pdf, last updated 25 August 2005.

Chapter 8
Conclusion

138. See Susan B. Glasser, "Putin Angered by Critics on Siege; West Fails to Grasp Situation, He Says," *Washington Post* (September 8, 2004), A1.

139. David E. Long, *The Anatomy of Terrorism*. New York: Free Press, 1990, p. 15.

140. On the concept of risk factors, see Stern, *Terror in the Name of God*, pp. 283–288.

141. Crenshaw, "The Causes of Terrorism," p. 385.

142. See Mia M. Bloom, "Palestinian Suicide Bombing: Public Support, Market Share and Outbidding," *Political Science Quarterly* 119:1 (Spring 2004).

143. See Lucy S. Dawidowicz, *The War Against the Jews: 1933–1945*. New York: Bantam Books, 1986.

Alexander, Yonah, David Carlton, and Paul Wilkinson, eds. *Terrorism: Theory and Practice.* Boulder, CO: Westview Press, 1979.

Allison, Graham. *Nuclear Terrorism: The Ultimate Preventable Catastrophe.* New York: Times Books/Henry Holt, 2004.

Anonymous. *Through Our Enemies' Eyes.* Washington, D.C.: Brassey's, 2003.

Anonymous. *Imperial Hubris: Why the West Is Losing the War on Terror.* Washington, D.C.: Brassey's, 2004.

Barber, Benjamin R. *Jihad vs. McWorld: Terrorism's Challenge to Democracy.* New York: Ballantine Books, 1996.

Bloom, Mia. *Dying to Kill: The Allure of Suicide Terror.* New York: Columbia University Press, 2005.

Burke, Jason. *Al Qaeda: Casting a Shadow of Terror.* New York: I.B. Tauris, 2003.

Crenshaw, Martha, ed. *Terrorism, Legitimacy and Power.* Middletown, CT: Wesleyan University Press, 1983.

Crenshaw, Martha, ed. *Terrorism in Context.* University Park, PA: Pennsylvania State University Press, 1995.

Freedman, Lawrence Z., and Yonah Alexander, eds. *Perspectives of Terrorism.* Wilmington, DE: Scholarly Resources, 1983.

Friedman, Thomas L. *The Lexus and the Olive Tree*, 2nd ed. New York: Anchor Books, 2000.

Gopin, Marc. *Between Eden and Armaggedon: The Future of World Religions, Violence, and Peacemaking.* New York: Oxford University Press, 2000.

Gunaratna, Rohan. *Inside Al Qaeda: Global Network of Terror.* New York: Columbia University Press, 2002.

Hertzberg, Hendrik. "Tuesday and After." *The New Yorker* (September 24, 2001).

Hoffman, Bruce. *Inside Terrorism.* New York: Columbia University Press, 1998.

Howard, Russell D., and Reid L. Sawyer. *Terrorism and Counterterrorism: Understanding the New Security Environment.* Guilford, CT: McGraw-Hill, 2003.

Huntington, Samuel. *Political Order in Changing Societies.* New Haven, CT: Yale University Press, 1968.

Janis, Irving L. *Victims of Groupthink: A Psychological Study of Foreign-Policy Decisions and Fiascoes.* Boston: Houghton Mifflin, 1972.

Juergensmeyer, Mark. *Terror in the Mind of God: The Global Rise of Religious Violence.* Berkeley, CA: University of California Press, 2001.

Kaldor, Mary. *New and Old Wars: Organized Violence in a Global Era.* Stanford, CA: Stanford University Press, 1999.

Laqueur, Walter. *The Age of Terrorism.* Boston: Little, Brown, 1987.

Laqueur, Walter. *No End to War: Terrorism in the 21st Century.* New York: Continuum, 2004.

Lesser, Ian O., et al. *Countering the New Terrorism.* Santa Monica, CA: RAND, 1999.

Li, Quan, and Drew Schaub, "Economic Globalization and Transnational Terrorism: A Pooled Time-Series Analysis." *Journal of Conflict Resolution* 48:2 (April 2004).

Lifton, Robert Jay. *Destroying the World to Save It: Aum Shinrikyo, Apocalyptic Violence, and the New Global Terrorism.* New York: Owl Books, 1999.

Long, David E. *The Anatomy of Terrorism.* New York: Free Press, 1990.

Moghadam, Assaf. "Palestinian Suicide Terrorism in the Second Intifada: Motivations and Organizational Aspects." *Studies in Conflict and Terrorism* 26:2 (March/April 2003).

National Commission on Terrorist Attacks Upon the United States. *The 9/11 Commission Report: Final Report of the National Commission on Terrorist Attacks Upon the United States,* Authorized Edition. New York: W.W. Norton, 2004.

Pillar, Paul. *Terrorism and U.S. Foreign Policy.* Washington, D.C.: Brookings Institution, 2001.

Radu, Michael. "The Futile Search for Root Causes of Terrorism." Foreign Policy Research Institute (FPRI) E-Note (April 23, 2002).

Rapoport, David C., ed. *Inside Terrorist Organizations.* New York: Frank Cass, 1988.

Reich, Walter. *Origins of Terrorism: Psychologies, Ideologies, Theologies, States of Mind.* Washington, D.C.: Woodrow Wilson Center Press, 1998.

Rotberg, Robert I., ed. *When States Fail: Causes and Consequences.* Princeton, NJ: Princeton University Press, 2004.

Russell, Charles, and Bowman Miller. "Profile of a Terrorist." *Terrorism: An International Journal* 1:1 (1977).

Sageman, Marc. *Understanding Terror Networks.* Philadelphia: University of Pennsylvania Press, 2004.

Schiff, Zeev, and Ehud Yaari. *Intifada—The Palestinian Uprising: Israel's Third Front.* New York: Simon & Schuster, 1989.

Snow, Donald. *Uncivil Wars: International Security and the New Internal Conflicts.* Boulder, CO: Lynne Rienner, 1996.

Sprinzak, Ehud. "The Psychological Formation of Extreme Left Terrorism in a Democracy: The Case of the Weathermen." In *Origins of Terrorism*, edited by Walter Reich. Washington, D.C.: Woodrow Wilson Center Press, 1998.

Stern, Jessica. *The Ultimate Terrorists.* Cambridge, MA: Harvard University Press, 1999.

Stern, Jessica. *Terror in the Name of God: Why Religious Militants Kill.* New York: Ecco/Harper Collins, 2003.

Taylor, Maxwell, and Ethel Quayle. *Terrorist Lives.* New York: Brassey's, 1994.

United Nations Development Programme. *Arab Human Development Report 2003.* New York: United Nations Development Programme, 2003.

U.S. Department of State. *Patterns of Global Terrorism 2003.* Washington, D.C.: United States Department of State, 2004.

Wilkinson, Paul. *Political Terrorism.* New York: John Wiley & Sons, 1972.

Wilson, James Q. *Political Organizations.* New York: Basic Books, 1973.

Zartman, William. *Collapsed States.* Boulder, CO: Lynne Rienner, 1995.

BOOKS

Abu-Amr, Ziad. *Islamic Fundamentalism in the West Bank and Gaza: Muslim Brotherhood and Islamic Jihad.* Bloomington, IN: Indiana University Press, 1994.

Abuza, Zachary. *Militant Islam in Southeast Asia: Crucible of Terror.* Boulder, CO: Lynne Rienner, 2003.

Arquilla, John, and David F. Ronfeldt. *The Advent of Netwar.* Santa Monica, CA: RAND, 1996.

Benjamin, Daniel, and Steven Simon. *The Age of Sacred Terror.* New York: Random House, 2002.

Bergen, Peter. *Holy War, Inc.: Inside the Secret World of Osama bin Laden.* New York: Free Press, 2001.

Clarke, Richard A. *Against All Enemies: Inside America's War on Terror.* New York: Free Press, 2004.

Fanon, Frantz. *The Wretched of the Earth.* New York: Grove Press, 1968.

Heymann, Philip B. *Terrorism and America: A Commonsense Strategy for a Democratic Society.* Cambridge, MA: MIT Press, 1998.

Hoffman, Bruce. "Al Qaeda, Trends in Terrorism, and Future Potentialities: An Assessment." *Studies in Conflict and Terrorism* 26:6 (November 2003).

Juergensmeyer, Mark. *The New Cold War? Religious Nationalism Confronts the Secular State.* Berkeley, CA: University of California Press, 1993.

Laquer, Walter. *The New Terrorism: Fanaticism and the Arms of Mass Destruction.* Oxford, UK: Oxford University Press, 1999.

Marty, Martin E., and R. Scott Appleby, eds. *Accounting for Fundamentalisms: The Dynamic Character of Movements.* Chicago: University of Chicago Press, 1994.

Marty, Martin E., and R. Scott Appleby. *The Glory and the Power: The Fundamentalist Challenge to the Modern World.* Boston, MA: Beacon Press, 1992.

Mishal, Shaul, and Sela, Avraham. *The Palestinian Hamas: Vision, Violence, and Coexistence.* New York: Columbia University Press, 2000.

Peters, Rudolph. *Jihad in Classical and Modern Islam.* Princeton, NJ: Markus Weiner Publishers, 1996.

Rashid, Ahmed. *Taliban: Militant Islam, Oil, and Fundamentalism in Central Asia.* New Haven, CT: Yale University Press, 2000.

Sprinzak, Ehud. *Brother Against Brother: Violence and Extremism in Politics from Altalena to the Rabin Assassination.* New York: Free Press, 1999.

Stohl, Michael, ed. *The Politics of Terrorism.* New York: Marcel Dekker, 1988.

WEBSITES

"The 9/11 Commission Report"
http://www.9-11commission.gov/report/911Report.pdf

Central Intelligence Agency (CIA), "War on Terrorism"
http://www.cia.gov/terrorism/index.html

Federal Bureau of Investigation (FBI) Counterterrorism Webpage
http://www.fbi.gov/terrorinfo/counterrorism/waronterrorhome.htm

FBI Most Wanted Terrorists
http://www.fbi.gov/mostwant/terrorists/fugitives.htm

International Policy Institute for Counter-Terrorism (ICT), Interdisciplinary Center, Herzliyya, Israel
http://www.ict.org.il

National Memorial Institute for the Prevention of Terrorism (MIPT) Terrorism Knowledge Base
http://www.tkb.org/Home.jsp

South Asia Terrorism Portal
http://www.satp.org

Terrorism Questions and Answers, Council on Foreign Relations
http://www.terrorismanswers.org

United States Department of Homeland Security
http://www.dhs.gov

United States Department of State, Patterns of Global Terrorism
http://www.state.gov/s/ct/rls/pgtrpt

page:

2: Associated Press, AP/Chao Soi Cheong
15: © Getty Images
24: © Bettmann/CORBIS
31: © Reuters/CORBIS
38: © Bettmann/CORBIS
60: Associated Press, AP/Nasser Nasser
71: © Peter Turnley/CORBIS
76: Associated Press, AP/IRAQI NEWS AGENCY

79: Associated Press, AP/Nadia Cohen
88: Associated Press, AP/Hagop Toranian
95: © Peter Turnley/CORBIS
105: © Peter Turnley/CORBIS
112: Associated Press, AP
119: © VIKTOR KOROTAYEV/Reuters/ CORBIS

Cover: David Caulkin AP/Wide World Photos

CONTRIBUTORS

ASSAF MOGHADAM is a Research Fellow at the Belfer Center for Science and International Affairs at Harvard University's John F. Kennedy School of Government and a doctoral candidate in international relations at The Fletcher School at Tufts University. Mr. Moghadam served as a consultant for Harvard University's Weatherhead Center for International Affairs (WCFIA), and has held various research positions at the Center for Strategic and International Studies (CSIS), the Center for Nonproliferation Studies, and the Washington Institute for Near East Policy. Mr. Moghadam has lectured on terrorism and suicide attacks before various audiences in the United States, Europe, and the Middle East. He is the author of *A Global Resurgence of Religion?* (Cambridge, Mass.: Weatherhead Center for International Affairs, 2003), and his research has been published in *Studies in Conflict and Terrorism*, the *Middle East Review of International Affairs*, and other scholarly journals.

The author would like to thank Kieran Brenner and Mia Bloom for their helpful comments.

LEONARD WEINBERG is Foundation Professor of Political Science at the University of Nevada. Over the course of his career he has been a Fulbright senior research fellow for Italy, a visiting fellow at the National Security Studies Center (University of Haifa), a visiting scholar at UCLA, a guest professor at the University of Florence, and the recipient of an H. F. Guggenheim Foundation grant for the study of political violence. He has also served as a consultant to the United Nations Office for the Prevention of Terrorism (Agency for Crime Control and Drug Prevention). For his work in promoting Christian–Jewish reconciliation Professor Weinberg was a recipient of the 1999 Thornton Peace Prize.

WILLIAM L. EUBANK is a graduate of the University of Houston, where he earned two degrees (B.S. and M.A.) in political science. He received his Ph.D. from the University of Oregon in 1978. Before coming to the University of Nevada, he taught briefly at California State University Sonoma and Washington State University. While at the University of Nevada, he has taught undergraduate courses in Constitutional Law, Civil Rights & Liberties, Political Parties and Elections, and graduate seminars in American Politics, the History of Political Science and Research Methods. The author or co-author of articles and papers in areas as diverse as statistics, research design, voting, and baseball, among other subjects, he is interested in how political violence (and terrorism) function as markers for political problems confronting governments.